ROAD RACING
& PREPARATION

ROAD CAR
RACING
& PREPARATION

TERRY GRIMWOOD

OSPREY

Published in 1989 by Osprey Publishing Limited
59 Grosvenor Street, London W1X 9DA

British Library Cataloguing in Publication Data

Grimwood, Terry
Road Car Racing and Preparation.
    1. Cars. Racing
    I. Title
    796.7'2
ISBN 0–85045–792–0

Printed and bound in Great Britain by
Butler & Tanner Ltd, Frome and London

*We would like to thank Neil Eason Gibson of the
RAC Motor Sports Association for detailed checking of the manuscript. His comments and help have
been invaluable.*

Contents

Introduction

With everyday motoring becoming more and more expensive, and the plague of sponsorship pushing the cost of motor sport higher and higher, fewer people are able to afford the luxury of a decent everyday road car *and* a separate car for weekend motor sport. Yet with car registrations up every year and motor club membership on the increase, more people than ever want to take part in some form of motor sport.

These factors, combined with the variety of genuinely high performance road cars now available from the mainstream motor industry, explain the significant increase over the last few years in the number of motor sport series available to drivers of ordinary road cars. Of course, some of these series have existed for many years, but they have been joined by many new classes and championships with the result that today's amateur competitor has a bewildering range of motor sport to choose from.

This book aims to cut through some of the confusion that exists and provide a usable guide to competing in motor sport with everyday road cars. The categories detailed here can all be tackled competitively in cars that can genuinely double up as day-to-day transport. I make that point because there are some categories of the sport that on the surface would appear to fit the bill but in reality are so specialized or so demanding that the amateur competitor with a dual-role car would find himself spending an awful lot of money only to be hopelessly outclassed.

A form of motor sport which requires no car preparation whatsoever does not exist; all the categories covered in this book are controlled by the RAC Motor Sport Association which demands that at the very least the cars should comply with certain basic requirements concerning safety. Nevertheless, many of the categories included in this book require

the barest minimum of preparation and expense, and some of them boast almost negligible running costs. The circuit racing championships are probably the most expensive, but even then there are classes available which provide the cheapest and most accessible motor racing you are ever going to find.

In addition to giving details of the many forms of motor sport available to the enthusiast with a suitable road car at his disposal, this book also steers the novice through the maze of club membership, licences, paperwork and car preparation. It even explains how to go about sorting the car's suspension to make it handle better and how to find out more about the techniques of competition driving.

I hope that with this book I can encourage you to stop dreaming and have a go yourself; I hope it will assist you in making the transition from armchair enthusiast to motor sport competitor. After all, if you can afford a road car you can afford to compete in it.

See you on the track.

Terry Grimwood

The author would like to thank the photographic staff of Cars & Car Conversions *magazine, plus Chris Harvey, Peter Chrisp and Keith Seume, for their invaluable assistance in assembling the photos and data for this book.*

Above right **Terry Grimwood overtaking Peter Dron in a journalist's race at Brands Hatch**

Below right **Terry Grimwood racing a roadgoing Sunbeam Talbot at Mallory Park**

1

Background

Motor sport and the RAC MSA

Motor sport in this country isn't merely a random collection of like-minded enthusiasts each concerned with his own particular interests and free to devise whatever regulations or operating practices he may desire. If this were the case anarchy would rule and there would soon be a public outcry if due attention was not given to matters of safety and public nuisance.

The vast majority of motor sport in this country comes under the control of the Royal Automobile Club Motor Sports Association Ltd (RAC MSA), and is recognized in this capacity by the World governing body, the Fédération Internationale de l'Automobile (FIA). The RAC MSA controls all the 'conventional' types of motor sport in Great Britain and is responsible for setting rules and regulations, issuing permits and licences, and policing the events which come under its sanction. Some categories of motor sport operate independently of the RAC, though these are dwindling in numbers and are largely restricted to some forms of grasstrack racing and short-oval racing; competitors taking part in these 'outlaw' events are not permitted to hold an RAC MSA competition licence, and any RAC MSA licence holder found to have participated in unsanctioned events risks having his licence suspended.

Given the level of influence that the RAC MSA wields, the single most important item of equipment in the would-be competitor's armoury is a copy of the RAC MSA Yearbook, known to one and all as the *Blue Book*; not surprisingly, all things considered, its cover is coloured blue, and it is published every year. The *Blue Book* is a mine of essential information, covering as it does everything to do with the organization and governing of motor sport. You will find it referred to constantly throughout this book.

The most relevant section for anyone considering preparing a car for any category of officially recognized motor sport is the Technical Regulations, which lays down in extreme detail everything you can and can't do to your car for the different sectors of the sport.

First there are the general regulations which apply to all vehicles regardless of type or purpose, then there are the more specific requirements which relate to particular categories, namely Autocross, Autotests, Cross Country and 4WD, Drag Racing, Hillclimbs and Sprints, Racing, Rallying, Rallycross, and finally Trials.

For information on competition licences and how to obtain the *Blue Book* see Chapter 2.

Given the incredible volume of motor sport that takes place every year in the UK it is not possible for the RAC MSA to organize every single event so certain other clubs are recognized by the MSA for the organization of motor competitions. In other words, while the MSA sets the framework and rules within which all competition must take place, it then delegates much of the organization of these events to motor clubs which comply with the MSA requirements and standards. Most of these are local clubs which deal with events taking place within their local geographic area, but there are a number of clubs operating on a national basis and involved in organizing competitions across the country. The advantage of joining one of these national clubs is a) they tend to organize a high number of events per year and run a wide variety of championships, and b) members of these clubs also tend to be invited as a matter of course to events organized by the smaller local clubs, whereas the reverse is seldom the case.

Thus the hierarchy of motor clubs in this country is as follows:

1 The RAC Motor Sport Association.
2 National Motor Clubs.
3 Local Motor Clubs.

Motor sport definitions

There are many different categories of motor sport, some with ambiguous or misleading names. The following is a list of the most common categories, excluding those unsuitable for roadgoing cars, with a brief rundown of their main characteristics:

Autocross Off-road racing against the clock, usually on fairly level surfaces such as grassy fields but the terrain can sometimes get chewed up and pretty rough. Cars usually start in pairs at 30-second intervals so an element of car-to-car dicing often takes place even though finishing position is irrelevant. Most autocross cars are stripped down and highly-tuned racers, but rally and road car classes will suit the roadgoing enthusiast.

RAC Speed licence required. Crash helmet required.

Autotests Reckoned to be one of the cheapest forms of motor sport available, it involves complicated manœuvres around marker cones (pylons), with much use of the handbrake and a great deal of tyre smoke. Looks easy, but certainly isn't – remembering the route of each test is hard enough, let alone mastering the technique of the 'reverse flick' so beloved of autotesters. Autotests require flat tarmac or concrete surfaces – most common venues are large car parks. Although basically cheap – no special preparation of the car is necessary – there can be a toll in tyres and transmissions.

No licence required except for championship events, which need RAC Clubman, Speed or Rally licence.

Circuit races What grand prix drivers do. Massed starts on a closed metalled racetrack. Positions on the start grid are determined by practice times, and first past the flag at the end of the race is the winner. Can be horrendously expensive if you're not careful, but championships abound for the hard-up enthusiast with only his road car to play with. Read on. . . .

RAC Race licence required, with medical certificate. Crash helmet required.

Drag races Straight line blasts over a $\frac{1}{4}$ mile strip of tarmac, timed to fractions of a second. Cars start in pairs and although first past the post is usually the winner the clock is the real enemy. A lack of respect for transmissions and a slick gearchange technique is essential, and despite the big buck 1000 + bhp monsters stealing the limelight there are plenty of opportunities for road cars to compete. And they don't have to be American.

RAC Clubman, Speed or Race licence required. Crash helmet required.

Hillclimbs Commonly misunderstood by the layman, this has nothing to do with climbing muddy banks but a lot to do with zapping up closed sections of metalled road. Cars start singly and race against the clock, and the skill lies in smoothness and perfection of line as much as out-and-out power. Caters for a wide range of cars, from special Formula 1-type single-seaters to standard road cars, and while competition can be fierce the social side is deemed almost as important. A great sport for the family, with a picnic hamper sharing priority with the tool kit.

RAC Clubman or Speed licence required. Crash helmet required.

Production car trials and cross country trials Another very cheap introduction to motor sport. Production car trials (PCTs) are what your man in the street thinks a hillclimb is, i.e., climbing up muddy or grassy banks and wending a way between trees and other scenery in an effort to see who can get 'furthest cleanest'. And cleanest does not refer to the state of the car but to how far you can go without coming to a standstill or hitting one of the canes that mark the route. The winner is the driver with the least penalty points at the end of the day. A cross country trial is the same but much more difficult, requiring the use of a four-wheel-drive vehicle; classes such as 'non damaging' and 'road traffic vehicle' exist for the competitor who wants to have a four-wheel-drive vehicle left to go home in at the end of the day.

RAC Clubman or Rally licence required.

Rallies These take two main forms: road rallying and special stage rallying. In both cases each car carries a crew of two, the driver and co-driver/navigator. The cars compete on timed sections linked by public roads. On road rallies these sections are known as 'selectives' and are on metalled surfaces, while on special stage rallies they are called – wait for it – 'special stages', which are generally on loose surfaces such as farm tracks, forest trails, etc. Both types of event require an element of navigation, more so on road rallies. For the novice, road rallying is by far the best bet, as cars can be almost standard road vehicles with little in the way of special preparation. Also they are less likely to get damaged by rough terrain. On the other hand, most road rallies take place at night which can be very exhausting.

RAC Clubman or Rally licence required for the driver, Clubman, Navigator or Rally licence required for the co-driver/navigator.

Sprints A bit like hillclimbs except they are flat, and generally on a circuit-type course rather than a strip of road. Venues are sometimes racetracks or parts of racetracks, but more often tend to be airfields with the course marked out with cones. Racing is against the clock, and the range of cars taking place is similar to those competing in hillclimbs. Indeed, many motor clubs or associations of motor clubs (see Chapter 2) run their own 'speed' championships which take in a mixture of both sprints and hillclimbs.

RAC Clubman or Speed licence required. Crash helmet required.

Clauses and licences

2

Clubs and licences

If you want to play tennis, you join a tennis club and you play tennis. If you want to play cricket, you join a cricket club and you play cricket. But if you want to go motor racing, you ... ummm ... well, what do you do?

It is a question that baffles many a would-be motor racing ace to the extent that some don't even bother to try to find out. 'Motor racing? Oh no, that's not for the likes of me and you, laddie. You have to pass examinations and 'ave a funny-sounding foreign name that ends in 'i'. Nay, lad, come t'club with us for a good game of dominoes.'

Much of this confusion probably arises because people aren't educated about motor sport at a young age in the same way as they learn about football or cricket. By its very nature – the fact that you must be able to drive and hold a full driving licence before you can compete – motor racing is primarily a sport for adults, and adults are notoriously bad at making the effort to learn something new.

In actual fact, the way into motor sport differs very little from any other sport; your first step should always be to join a club. Most beginners tend to join their local motor club which will probably hold meetings once a week or so in a local pub or church hall. If you don't already know where your local club hangs out, the RAC Motor Sports Association has a register of clubs which are affiliated to the RAC so the answer is just a telephone call away. Your local library should also have details of motor clubs within your area.

There are also a number of regional associations consisting of anything up to a hundred or so local clubs banded together to form a more powerful organization for the purpose of organizing events or dealing with other motor sport bodies. Addresses and contact numbers for all these associations will be found at the end of this chapter. A letter or

telephone call to the association that covers your region should provide a list of at least half a dozen clubs not too far from where you live.

Apart from the important aspect of meeting and mixing with like-minded people who will be invaluable when it comes to guiding you in the right direction, it is also a legal requirement that you join some sort of club or organization before taking part in motor sport competition. If you are not keen on the idea of joining a local club, however, the only real alternative is to belong to one of the national motor sport clubs. These are the bodies that organize many of the major motor sport events in this country and you will normally need to be a member if you intend to take part in one of their meetings or championships unless it is an Open event or a Restricted/Clubman event to which your club has been invited. (The grading of events is explained in more detail further on.)

For circuit racing competitors there are three main national organizations: British Racing Drivers Club (BRDC) based at Silverstone; British Racing and Sports Car Club (BRSCC) based at Brands Hatch; British Automobile Racing Club (BARC) based at Thruxton. Other forms of motor sport have their own national bodies such as: British Trials and Rally Drivers Association (BTRDA) for rallies, trials and autotests; British Drag Racing Association (BDRA); and the Hillclimb and Sprint Association (HSA).

Less well known, perhaps, but particularly worthy of note for anyone interested in road car racing are two specialist clubs at the low-buck end of motor sport. The efforts of the 750 Motor Club have earned the respect of everyone in motor racing over the last few years. With well over 2000 members, the club is now a limited company offering excellent value for money membership and benefits. It also organizes its own Roadgoing Sports

Car Championship and Kit Car Championship with classes directly aimed at the amateur with limited resources, but run very much on a professional basis both in terms of organization and driving standards. You would also be hard pushed to find a friendlier, more accessible group of racing enthusiasts.

Similarly, the 96 Club is an excellent organization aimed at those who want to experience circuit driving without going to the expense of preparing their car to full RAC specification. Each year the club organizes around 15 private meetings at race circuits around the country where members can put their road car through its paces in relative safety without risking their licences. Members' cars range from standard saloons through to exoticars and roadracing machinery but there is no need for them to be modified to meet the RAC safety requirements normally demanded by the circuits for test sessions. That having been said, it's your car, and your neck, so a certain amount of self-restraint is called for!

Once you're a fully paid-up member of the organization of your choice and happily posing around town in your club tie, sweater and furry slippers, the next step on the road to superstardom is to apply for an RAC competition licence. This is a necessity for virtually all forms of motor sport unless you intend to take part only in small closed events organized by your local club, for which a club membership card will normally, but not always, be sufficient.

Application forms for an RAC licence are available direct from the RAC MSA in Slough, although it is always worth checking with your club secretary to see if he keeps a supply.

There are several types of licence available depending on the type of event you wish to take part in. An explanatory leaflet should arrive with your application form from the RAC but if you are still confused, check with the RAC before you return the form as subsequent changes usually cost extra.

You will also receive a blank medical certificate included in your application form and this must be completed if you intend to take part in any form of circuit racing; it is not a requirement for speed events such as drag racing, hillclimbs and sprints and autotests, or for rallying. If you are going circuit racing, though, you will need to make an appointment to see your doctor because the medical certificate can only be completed by a qualified medical practitioner.

The RAC medical examination is carried out to a standard similar to that for life insurance purposes but special attention is paid to such things as eyesight, heart condition, diabetes and epilepsy. Obviously it is all designed to ensure that at least you are fit to race and will not be a danger to yourself or others. Most doctors charge somewhere in the region of £25 for carrying out this service but there is no point in quibbling about the cost. This is very much a necessary expense because you definitely will not be allowed to take part in a circuit race without a properly completed medical certificate.

Events are graded in six stages, but only the first four will be relevant to anyone just starting out in motor sport. As we have already mentioned, a Closed event is open only to members of the organizing club but this tends to apply only to a few small autotests, trials and road rallies. The vast majority of events that interest you will fall within the Clubman or Restricted categories, which are virtually the same in that only members of the organizing club or other invited clubs can take part. National events are open to any *qualified* competitor licenced by the RAC MSA but not to holders of foreign licences. We stress the 'qualified' for reasons you will see in a moment.

Prices of licences vary depending on the status of the event for which they are valid but you should note that it is not always wise to opt for the cheapest and lowest grade of licence just because you are a beginner. For those events which require a Speed licence, namely autotests, drag races, hillclimbs, sprints and rallycross, you could opt for the cheaper Restricted Speed or, cheaper still, Clubman RS licence, but if you should then decide to take in a national event as your confidence grows, you will have to pay extra to upgrade your licence to National Speed. This will cost more than applying for a National Speed licence in the first place, so it pays to think ahead.

For racing and rallying events, however, it is not so simple because you *must* start with a Restricted Race or Restricted Rally licence which can only be upgraded by obtaining signatures from event officials to confirm that your driving was up to scratch in a specified number of events – hence the 'qualified' proviso for taking part in national events. In some cases, you may even have to finish in the top five or top ten on a number of occasions before you obtain sufficient signatures to upgrade, although more often it is simply a case of keeping your nose clean. Running fellow drivers off the road while screaming 'Geronimooooooo' is unlikely to do you any favours at this stage in the game. It might win you a few friends in the crowd but race stewards tend not to share their sense of humour.

If this all seems rather confusing at this point in time, don't worry. It is. But everything becomes much clearer when you have actually got all the relevant paperwork in front of you. Once you have decided which licence you need, filled in the forms and sent off your cheque, your licence should arrive within a couple of weeks accompanied by the RAC MSA Yearbook (or *Blue Book* as it is more commonly known). As soon as the licence arrives, sign it and affix a recent photograph of yourself.

If you're fortunate enough to have some form of sponsorship or financial backing for your racing, and if such support is permitted for your class of competition, there are two other forms of licence which need to be considered. An Entrant's licence must be obtained if you wish to have your entry listed in the programme in the name of an organization, firm or sponsor, or indeed any person other than the driver. The programme or results sheet must state the title or name of an entrant and/or driver exactly as it is stated on the appropriate licence; up to six words are permitted.

It is your responsibility to check that an Entrant's licence has been applied for – many companies will not even know that such a thing exists – and it could be that you will be expected to pay for it out of your sponsorship money. If your sponsor is already involved in motor sport, it is worth checking whether or not they already possess an Entrant's licence for other drivers; if they do, a copy is available from the RAC at nominal cost.

A Driver's and/or Entrant's licence permits a limited amount of advertising to be shown on the sides of the car but not facing forward, rearward or on the roof. This is limited to, on each side of the car, the name of the entrant in letters not exceeding $4\frac{1}{2}$ in.; the name of the driver in letters not exceeding 4 in.; the make of the car (or name of mechanic) in letters not exceeding $3\frac{1}{2}$ in.; a maximum of five decals, not exceeding 55 sq.in. each and which may not be linked to form a name or message. You must also make available to the organizer an area of 100 sq.in. on each side of the car, adjacent to your competition number space, to be used to promote a championship or event sponsor.

If additional advertising is required, you must buy an advertising permit which allows unlimited advertising and is available in three grades – Restricted, National and International. An advertising permit does not qualify as, or take the place of, an Entrant's licence and it can only be obtained by a competition licence holder. And beware – your sponsor might love the idea of your car being emblazoned in his corporate colours, but he might not be so keen to pay for it. Make sure they will cough up for the licence before you apply. And before you paint the car!

But don't forget to check the championship regulations to ensure that sponsorship and advertising are permitted.

Contacts

The RAC Motor Sports Association
Motor Sports House
Riverside Park
Colnbrook
Slough
Tel: 0753 681736

British Automobile Racing Club
Thruxton Circuit
Andover
Hants SP11 8PN
Tel: 0264 772696

British Drag Racing Association
Bakersfield
29 West Drive
Caldecote
Cambs CB3 7NY
Tel: 0954 210028

British Racing Drivers Club
Silverstone Circuit
Silverstone
Towcester
Northants NN12 8TN
Tel: 0327 857271

British Racing & Sports Car Club
Brands Hatch Circuit
Fawkham
Dartford
Kent DA3 8NH
Tel: 0474 874445

British Rallycross Drivers Association
21 Watermill Way
South Darenth
Kent DA4 9BB
Tel: 0622 863605

British Trial & Rally Drivers Association
19a Oxford Street
Lambourne
Berks RG16 7XS
Tel: 0488 72027

British Women Racing Drivers Club
Hollybush Cottage
Chapel Lane
Stoke Poges SL2 4QJ
Tel: 0753 654340

Hillclimb & Sprint Association
22 Silhill Hall Road
Solihull
W. Midlands B91 1JU
Tel: 021 454 6171 (B)

The 96 Club
11 Gloucester Road
London SW1
Tel: 01 584 9536

The 750 Motor Club Ltd
16 Woodstock Road
Witney
Oxon OX8 6DT
Tel: 0993 2285

Regional associations

Association of Central-Southern Motor Clubs
Secretary: Mrs L. Neal
60 Hillsboro Road
Bognor Regis
W. Sussex PO21 2DY
Tel: 0243 862326

Association of Eastern Motor Clubs
Secretary: D. A. James
11 Rowley Close
Wembley
Middx HA0 4HE
Tel: 01 902 6621

Association of Midland Motor Clubs
Secretary: J. Pick
37 School Road
Hall Green
Birmingham B28 8RG
Tel: 021 744 8522 (B)

Association of North-East and Cumbria Car Clubs
Secretary: K. Kirtly
12 Lamonby Close
Nunthorpe
Middlesbrough
Cleveland TS7 0QG
Tel: 0642 326682

Association of North-East Midland Motor Clubs
Secretary: J. B. Wilkinson
1 Bayons Avenue
Springfield
Grimsby
S. Humberside
DN33 3LN
Tel: Grimsby 59232 (B)
      Grimsby 79700 (H)

Association of Northern Car Clubs
Secretary: J. H. Richardson
67 West Park
Selby
N. Yorks YO8 0JN
Tel: 0757 702048 (H)

Association of Northern Ireland Car Clubs
Secretary: N. Moffitt
34 Jersey Avenue
Lisburn
Co. Antrim BT27 4BJ
Tel: 08462 3110 (H)

Association of North-Western Car Clubs
Secretary: A. Dean-Lewis
44 Penrhyn Isaf Road
Llandudno
N. Wales
Tel: 0492 81222 (B)
      0492 46688 (H)

Association of South Eastern Motor Clubs
Secretary: B. Elkington
62 Widmore Road
Bromley
Kent BR1 3BD
Tel: 01 464 2713 (H)
        01 698 4441 (B)

Association of South Western Motor Clubs
Secretary: R. B. Mayo
88 Queensholm Drive
Downend
Bristol
Tel: 0272 781111 × 4274 (B)
        0272 560114 (H)

Association of West Midlands Motor Clubs
Secretary: J. Arnold
Wharfe Cottage
Longdon on Tern
Telford
Shropshire TF6 6LQ
Tel: 0952 770211 (H)

Association of West Scotland Motor Sports Clubs
Secretary: D. Attwood
Jura
Larg Road
Stranraer
Tel: Stranraer 2666 (B)
        Stranraer 4791 (H)

East of Scotland Association of Car Clubs
I. Lawrie
27 Clermiston Road
Edinburgh EH12 6XD
Tel: 031 334 3190 (H)

East Midlands Association of Motor Clubs
Secretary: I. A. Dixon
11 Osberton Place
Hunters Bar
Sheffield S11 8XL
Tel: 0742 665510 (H)

London Counties Association of Motor Clubs
Secretary: A. Biss
6 Wavertree Road
South Woodford
London E18
Tel: 01 936 3137 (B)
        01 989 2515 (H)

The Welsh Association of Motor Clubs
Secretary: Ron Summerfield
'Llyswen'
20 Three Elms Road
Hereford HR4 0RH
Tel: 0432 273409 (H)

3

Choices

This part of the book looks at the various categories and classes of motor sport suitable for dual-purpose road cars. Each category is described in considerable detail so that you can decide whether or not your current car is suited to any particular discipline; alternatively you can select a category that has particular appeal, and then make a decision as to the best car for your needs.

Addresses are given at the end of each description to enable you to seek more information, or go right ahead and enrol with one of the organizing bodies.

References are made throughout this section to the RAC Motor Sport Association Year Book, sometimes referred to as the Technical Regulations but more often as the *Blue Book*. This is the bible for all motor sport competitors, and it is described in greater detail in Chapter 1.

If you do not as yet have a car – or have one that is not suitable for any of the categories covered in this book – then you would do well to give a great deal of thought to your eventual choice of car. If a one-make series appeals then your decision is virtually made; but even so, in categories such as the Porsche Series you have quite a wide choice of classes and models which makes your decision-making a bit more tricky.

Your first priority must be cost, and an acceptance of the fact that a Porsche 911 Turbo costs a mite more to buy and run than a 924.

Second, you should think very hard about your own experience (or lack of it) and capabilities. If your on-track experience is nil and your most powerful car to date an 850 Mini, then perhaps you should leave the Turbo until you have put a season or two's racing behind you.

Also take maintenance into consideration, and not just from the cost point of view. If you have limited mechanical ability and limited facilities, then steer clear of cars which demand both.

This matter of mechanical skill and workshop facilities is an important consideration when choosing a category of motor sport because all sections of the sport require some degree of preparation and if you have very limited resources at your disposal then you should steer clear of anything that requires a high level of preparation. Opt instead for something like autotests or production car trials, or perhaps sprints, in which very little work needs to be done to the car to make it ready for your first event. It is all too easy to set an unrealistic target and then find yourself with a part completed car blocking the driveway for the next two years.

In categories where a wide range of cars is permitted, the best way to decide on the car to use is to get along to an event and see what everyone else is using. And more importantly, see what's doing the winning; it may be that the championship leader is an absolute ace in a not so good car, but by and large you will get a fairly good idea of the cars to choose from. Then it comes down to personal appeal and your own instinct – but remember, if you choose a model of car that no one else is using (either because you're daft or because you reckon that you know something they don't), then there'll be no one else to pinch ideas from. And of course if you fail to feature in the results you won't know whether it's the car or your driving that needs looking at. A model of car with a proven track record will provide a far better yardstick by which to judge your driving skills.

If the category you choose is fairly new, or even inaugural, then studying form will not give you a very clear picture of the car to have. However, there are certain guidelines that should help you choose a suitable machine.

First, choose the category and class of racing that interests you. Then look at the regulations to see if there is a specified list of cars to choose from; if there isn't then you've got the whole output of the world's motor industry at your disposal. So now list the characteristics of your chosen category, and using whatever sources of information you can lay your hands on – motoring magazines, buyer's guides, manufacturers' literature – see which cars best match up with your list of requirements.

This detailing of characteristics is important because not every form of motor sport requires, for example, a 0–60 time of 5 seconds and a top speed of 180 mph, so the only reason for checking out performance lists is if you specifically need a high performance car.

For example, for autotests you might list your priorities as: all-round visibility; short wheelbase; front-wheel drive; good turning circle. In which case a Lamborghini Countach would be next to useless. Similarly, a VW Beetle may be ace for production car trials but hopeless on the racetrack.

In general it is fair to say that you can forget four- or five-door models, or estate cars. They are not only heavier but tend also to lack the necessary rigidity required for competition use.

Although outright power is not always a prime requirement, a good power/weight ratio usually is, for there are not many categories of motor sport that can be tackled successfully in an underpowered tank. So if you are looking at a particular model range choose the one that gives the best power/weight ratio. Simply divide the bhp of the car by its weight to give a bhp per ton (or kg) factor.

As mentioned earlier, ease of preparation could be a significant factor, along with the availability and cost of spares. If you work as a mechanic for a Ford dealer, for example, you might consider that using a Fiesta or Escort or Capri might have certain advantages over a Porsche or BMW!

The whole process of car selection reduces down to straight common sense. Once you have made a choice of the sort of motor sport that interests you then there is a mass of information available in one form or another to help you make your choice; the message here is, do not let your heart rule your head. Choose wisely and carefully, and avoid the trap of jumping at a particular model of car just because it has a momentary or impractical appeal.

Finally, be aware that regulations are constantly being changed by their organizing bodies so it is wise to obtain the latest information before preparing your car for any of the following categories.

Alfa Romeo racing

Those of you who delight in those distinctly Latin products of the Alfa Romeo factory will no doubt be delighted to learn of the 'Chris Knott Insurance Alfa Romeo Performance Cars Championship', a one-make series organized by the Alfa Romeo Owners' Club in conjunction with the ubiquitous BRSCC.

This series is open to any production or production-based Alfa Romeo, and within its Standard Production and Roadgoing Modified classes provides a genuine means of motor racing in the same car you use for day-to-day activities. The series tends to attract good grids and the racing can sometimes be *very* close indeed. The Alfa people tend to group together at race meetings and the atmosphere is therefore very clubby and supportive rather than oppressively competitive. Off the track, that is. . . .

The championship is run to regulations devised by the AROC and BRSCC and is divided into five separate classes:

Class A: Standard Production up to 1600 cc;
Class B: Standard Production over 1600 cc;

All Alfas are pretty sporty, and make wonderful road/race cars

Class C: Modified up to 1600 cc;
Class D: Modified over 1600 cc;
Class E: Roadgoing Modified.

As you can see, the Roadgoing Modified class has no capacity restrictions and falls somewhere between the Standard Production and Modified categories. It is therefore likely to appeal to the competitor who wants to go a bit quicker than the standard cars but also wishes to retain an acceptable degree of 'roadability'. The Modified categories are more for outright race cars and while it is theoretically possible to compete with a car that doubles up for road use, the practicality of doing so is questionable. However, for those who are interested the regulations are very similar to those listed for the Modified section of the Italian Inter-Marque Challenge detailed on p. 43, thus the regulations listed as follows are for the Standard and Roadgoing Modified categories only.

Below **If you have money to spend, you can modify your Alfa up to full race specification—the championship caters for all types**

Above **You can start with a standard Alfa and gradually develop it into an outright racer—still within the same championship**

The basic RAC MSA Technical Regulations for race cars must be complied with in all classes, as must the basic safety regulations. All cars must be fitted with at least a rear roll-cage, although a front cage is also strongly recommended. In addition a proper full race seat harness must be fitted, as must a minimum 1.5 kg fire extinguisher, electrical cutout switch and driver's head restraint. All good sensible stuff, designed to preserve life and limb so that motor racing can be safe as well as enjoyable.

Standard Production Classes A and B. For the purpose of these regulations the term 'standard' is considered by the AROC to mean 'as originally produced by the vehicle manufacturer', which seems clear enough. Although road tax and MoT certification are not prerequisites of the series it is expected that all the cars should be roadworthy and capable of passing an MoT test.

The chassis and bodywork specification must remain as standard except that interior trim and passenger seats can be removed; it is likely that those with genuine roadgoing cars will want to retain some semblance of civility within their cars, but it is perfectly possible to remove seats and carpet before a race and then put them back in again before the journey home.

The AROC accepts that there may be folk wishing to race in the Standard Production series using a car which has previously had the wheel-arches extended beyond standard. If this is the case then the modified arches may be retained but wheels no wider than 6 in. may be fitted, and spacers may not be used to fill the space. So if your car has been modified to take 10 in. wide rims (!) you'll just have to accept the fact that it will look a bit naff on wheels some 4 in. narrower, but at least you'll have the chance to race.

Standard Production cars must retain a minimum ground clearance of 4 in.

And so to engines. Hardly surprisingly the engine

must remain in the same location as standard for the car in question and all moving parts of the engine (which seems a clear enough definition) must remain standard and within the tolerances specified by the manufacturer. The same goes for compression ratio and port sizes.

The induction/fuel supply system must remain standard, and the exhaust manifold must be as supplied by the manufacturer – on the Alfasud the manifold is considered to be the part between the head and the first join in the exhaust system. Which doesn't leave a lot you can do except that on the Alfasud you are permitted to change the carburettors and linkage for another type of Weber or Dellorto provided that the carburettor body and choke sizes remain the same, i.e. maximum 32 mm chokes in a 36 mm body.

Other than that the fitment of an oil cooler is about all you can do to the engine, although you can fit transistorized ignition should you wish.

Moving on to suspension, you can change the dampers and springs (provided the diameter remains the same) but solid suspension top mounts and replacement Nylon bushes or Rose joints are not allowed, and Alfasud torsion bars must not be more than 23.5 mm thick. That does not leave a vast amount of scope but enough to give improved handling and roadholding without making the car a pig on ordinary roads.

Virtually everything else on the car must remain standard, except that brake linings and hose can be uprated and a proper racing fuel tank, while not mandatory, is permitted. Also mechanical components may be regarded as interchangeable within each model range (other than the GTA in the 105 series) which would allow the Giulia Super to run in Class B as a 2-litre, or a late series Alfasud 1.5 to be fitted with an earlier 1.2 Ti gearbox.

As mentioned earlier the maximum rim width is 6 in. and the AROC encourages the use of wheels with a standard appearance. Tyres must be road tyres from the RAC MSA Technical Regulations QP 3.1 List 1, Tyres For Production Saloon and Sports Car racing. This list tends to be updated on an annual basis so it does not pay to assume that the tyre doing all the winning one year will remain eligible for the next, although the RAC MSA do endeavour to give ample forewarning of any likely changes to the list.

Now it could be that the strictly limited specification of the Standard Production classes is a shade mundane for your tastes, or maybe you already have an Alfa that has been subjected to the kind of tuning which makes it ineligible for the Production class. Which is where we come to the next section, designated Class E.

Roadgoing Modified This class differs from Classes A and B in a number of ways, not the least being a rather more liberal attitude towards engine tuning. In fact anything goes provided that the type of engine for the model concerned is not altered and fuel injection or turbocharging is only allowed where it is part of the engine's original standard specification. Supercharging is banned completely.

As far as suspension is concerned the same principle applies, in that any modifications are acceptable provided that the original suspension method remains. If you intend using coil spring/damper units ('coilovers') on the Alfetta front suspension the standard torsion bar must remain in place and operational.

Given that you can do a lot more to make the Class E cars quicker it is not surprising that wider wheel rims are permitted, albeit only 1 in. wider at 7 in. However, the same tyre restrictions apply as for the Standard Production classes, and you will have to consult good old List 1 to make your selection.

With the tightly controlled Standard Production classes and the more liberal Roadgoing Modified and Modified classes the AROC and BRSCC have created a racing championship that will appeal to a wide range of Alfa Romeo enthusiasts, and which provides the opportunity to try out these unashamedly sporty cars in their historically natural environment. The series is professionally run and there is a wide variety of awards, including a Handicap Challenge and a Ladies' Award.

Licence required: Restricted Race with medical certificate.

Series co-ordinator: Michael Lindsay, Alfa Romeo Owners Club Ltd, 97 High Street, Linton, Cambs CB1 6JT. Tel: 0223 891219 (Tuesday to Friday, afternoons only).

Club membership required: Alfa Romeo Owners Club (address above) and The BRSCC, Brands Hatch Circuit, Fawkham, Dartford, Kent DA3 8NH. Tel: 0474 874445.

Astra/Nova Challenge

This is a rather unusual category in that it is a strictly two-make series that combines eight forestry rallies with two tarmac events.

The Challenge is heavily supported by the Vauxhall/Opel Dealer Sport network, with a comprehensive back-up and support scheme offering advice for everything from car preparation to sponsorship and PR promotion. As such, it is perhaps a bit more professional than many other categories discussed in this book and will demand a little more in terms of competitive 'edge' from its competitors. You can certainly compete in a car which doubles up as everyday transport, but you will inevitably find yourself up against many competitors whose cars are used solely for competition purposes, and who as a result are prepared to be that much more competitive. However, that shouldn't matter if the name of your particular game is to compete for the sake of it rather than to be a superstar.

Included within the overall Astra-Nova Challenge is a Junior Cup open to all competitors under 25 years of age, and a Ladies' Award.

Because of the heavy support this series receives there is a considerable prize fund available; for example, in the admittedly unlikely possibility of a female driver aged under 25 winning every rally, both races and the special Press and PR Award, she would scoop no less than £8000 during the year, which is no mean amount.

As the title suggests the Challenge is open to Vauxhall Astra and Nova cars. In addition, Opel Kadetts are eligible in the Astra category and Opel Corsas in the Nova category. The cars can be any saloon or hatchback configuration but all must use the General Motor 'Family One' 1300S ohc engine.

As it is the Vauxhall Opel dealers who between them put up the prize funds and underwrite the administration of the series, each competing car must be allied to a Vauxhall Opel dealer; this may merely be in name only, or the individual dealer may be persuaded to provide extra support in terms of, for example, cheap parts, workshop facilities,

The Challenge is supported by the Vauxhall/Opel Dealer Sport network

help with transport or, of course, direct cash sponsorship.

Each competitor must register for the Challenge, and will receive a livery pack of Astra-Nova Challenge stripes and championship decals.

All the rallies qualifying for the Challenge are also rounds of the BTRDA Gold Star Rally Championship, with the Astra-Novas competing in a separate category within each event; A-N competitors can also score points in the up-to-1300 cc class of the Gold Star Championship.

Throughout the year a number of seminar/tuition sessions take place around the country, with advice on preparation, driving and co-driving.

The regulations The full technical regulations are available in an impressive information manual provided by the organizers. This manual contains everything the would-be competitor is likely to need to know before taking part in his first event.

Basically the cars are based on FIA Group A Regulations, and all cars must comply with certain specified sections of the RAC Technical Regulations, particularly those concerned with safety.

The Challenge is open to 1300 Astras, Novas and Opels

Although the bodyshell must remain essentially standard extra metal may be added for strengthening purposes – very necessary for special stage rallying – provided it follows the existing shape and contours of the car.

Inside, insulation may be removed, along with carpets, headlinings, rear seats and rear parcel shelf. The original front seats can be replaced with competition seats provided a headrest is fitted to each seat. Decorative strip outside the car may be dispensed with, while certain add-on spoilers and side skirts may be fitted if required. Glass sunroofs are not allowed, and the windscreen must be of the laminated type.

Engine modifications are very limited, being restricted primarily to balancing internal components and fitting a modified standard cylinder head. Even so, head modifications are restricted to port sizes as laid down by the regulations (drawings are supplied), and valves must not exceed 33 mm inlet, 29 mm exhaust, with an overall valve length of 105 mm.

An uprated oil pump is permitted, but only if its installation doesn't involve machining the block, and while it is accepted that a block rebore may be necessary a bore maximum of 75.08 mm must not be exceeded.

When talking about exhaust and inlet manifolds the information manual uses the wonderful word 'fettled', stating that manifolds may be fettled but specified orifice sizes must not be exceeded. Couldn't have put it better myself.

Moving to suspension, the standard system must be retained but may be modified by fitting uprated springs, anti-roll bars, competition bushes and protective 'skids' to the suspension arms. There is an uprated shock aborber kit – the Bilstein 'Challenge' shock absorber kit – available to registered competitors at a special price. In addition, the front suspension strut casing assembly can be strengthened by welding in webs to stop them bending.

A higher ratio steering rack is allowed – of huge benefit on a rally car – and the steering wheel type is free as long as it incorporates a horn operable by the driver; in addition a foot-operated horn must be provided for the co-driver.

Any type of clutch is allowed – but only if the same number of plates as the original are retained. As far as the gearbox is concerned you can only use the General Motors F10 unit, and the organizers provide a list of gear ratios and final drive ratios that may be used; if they're not listed you can't fit them.

As far as brakes are concerned the ventilated front discs off GTE models may be fitted, while rear drums can remain standard or be filched from the Astra/Kadett 1600/1800 model or the Estate/Van variant. An alternative pedal box is allowed, as is that delight of rally drivers the world over – the adjustable brake balance adjuster.

Wheels must be 13 in. diameter × 5.5 in wide, but other than that they are free – which is not the case with the tyres, which must be Colway Rally Plus in either 155 or 165 sizes for the forestry events, and Avon Turbospeeds for the two tarmac rallies. In both cases the tyres are available at a special price to registered competitors, and in the case of the former a Colway tyres mobile fitting unit attends all rallies to provide a free fitting service.

The Astra-Nova Challenge may not be the cheapest way of starting off in motor sport, but it provides a taste of commercialism that some competitors might relish, and by sharing events with the BTRDA Gold Star series it also provides a useful comparison with a more professional level of rallying. Inasmuch as it requires drivers to hold a National Rally licence it is more suited to the competitor with some experience behind him than the complete novice.

Licence required: National Rally licence for driver and co-driver.

Series co-ordinator: Andrew Duerden, Hadley House, Great Glen, Leics LE8 0GN, Tel: 053 759 2640.

Club membership required: British Trials and Rally Drivers Association (BTRDA), Ron Crellin, 6 The Moorings, Colwich, Staffs, Tel: 021 336 5208 (B), 0889 882168 (H).

Autocross

This is a good 'clubbie' class of motor racing, ideal for those who like doing it in the dirt but don't want to spend the small fortune it costs to go rallycrossing. Autocross is no longer as hugely popular as it was in the heyday of the Players No 6 Championship in the early 1970s, but nevertheless it enjoys considerable popularity on a local level.

The British Trials and Rally Drivers Association (BTRDA) (see Chapter 2) organizes a Nationwide Autocross Championship which rather neatly gives competitors the opportunity of competing in a national series without the expense of lots of travel. The BTRDA manages this by nominating up to 28 local autocrosses around the country – each run by a local motor club – but requiring only the best ten timed runs to count towards the Championship. And as each competitor gets two timed runs at each event, you only need to compete in five events to qualify for the Championship. Of course, you can do as many rounds as you like in order to improve your 'best 10' rating – or just for the fun of it – but you can nevertheless choose only the rounds closest to you that require the least travelling.

At the end of the season there is a National Final – the only time when all competitors need to get together – with each driver getting three timed runs, the best two of which are added to his season total to determine final Championship positions.

Thus the BTRDA have very cleverly managed to combine the economic benefits of local competition with the prestige of a National Championship.

Autocross events take place on unsealed surfaces – for which read 'fields' – and competitors race against the clock, although they are generally started in pairs to make life a little more exciting! Each timed run usually comprises the start lap, one flying lap and the finish lap.

Although many autocross cars are very specialized machines there are three BTRDA classes reserved for roadgoing cars:

Class G: Rally and road cars 1301 cc to 1650 cc;
Class H: Rally and road cars 1651 cc and over;
Class J: Rally and road cars up to 1300 cc.

The reason for the odd order is that Class J is a BTRDA class added to the existing RAC nominated classes.

Below **Autocross can get a bit bumpy, so a sumpguard is a wise precaution**

Above **Rally cars can double up as autocrossers, and make great all-round road/competition machines**

In all three classes the vehicles must be taxed, tested and insured for the road, and comply with all other laws relating to vehicles on public roads.

All cars must also comply with Section QA of the RAC MSA *Blue Book*, which covers the general prescriptions for all vehicles competing in motor sport regardless of their classification. The main items for consideration are: fireproof bulkheads between driver and engine and driver and fuel tank; battery protection to prevent acid leaks; the battery earth strap clearly marked with yellow markings; and no wheel spacers wider than 1 in.

In addition, Section QB of the *Blue Book* covers regulations specific to autocross cars; however, many of the things mentioned – such as lightweight body panels, no windscreens, etc. are not permitted in the roadgoing classes anyhow. You don't even have to fit a roll-over bar, and although you are strongly advised to do so this does mean that you can compete in your road car without the intrusion of a roll-cage, which can sometimes be a bit of a nuisance in everyday use. It also enables you to have an exploratory crack at autocross to see how you like it, without too much initial expense.

What you do need to have is the ignition cut-off switch (normally the ignition key) clearly marked ON–OFF, and it does no harm to have the location of the ignition cut-off switch written on the driver's door – e.g. 'IGNITION ON COLUMN' – so that the marshals can find it in a hurry if they need to. A circuit breaker switch mounted in front of the windscreen and identified by a red spark on a blue triangle is recommended, but not compulsory.

As far as seatbelts are concerned you can get away with ordinary lap and diagonals, but if you are at all serious about your racing you will want a full harness.

A fire extinguisher is compulsory, minimum 2.5 kg capacity, mounted in the cockpit of the car within easy reach of the driver. And, of course, all drivers must wear crash helmets complying with RAC MSA regulations (see Chapter 4).

The windscreen must be of laminated glass.

Tuning is left up to the individual, the main restriction being how much of the car's practicality you wish to retain. Engine, transmission, brakes, wheels are all unrestricted, and you can also dispose of all the interior trim and passenger seats if you wish. Don't expect many friends to want to take a ride with you, though!

Many local motor clubs are involved with autocross, and most Associations of Motor Clubs run their own particular championships as well as hosting qualifying rounds of the BTRDA series. As such, autocross is one of the most accessible forms of off-road motor sport.

Licence required: Clubman RS, Rally or Speed.

Club membership required: Local motor club membership and/or BTRDA membership. BTRDA membership secretary: Liz Cox, 19a Oxford Street, Lambourne, Berks RG16 7XS. Tel: 0488 72027.

Further information: BTRDA Autocross Committee secretary, Robin Morris, Penn Moor Farm, Chamberlains Lane, Penn, Wolverhampton, W. Midlands.

Autotests

The ideal sport for those who have mastered the intricacies of the local Sainsbury's car park, autotests involve car handling and manoeuvring of the highest order. Deceptively simple, autotesting requires tremendous concentration, lightning reflexes and absolute familiarity with the dimensions and handling characteristics of your car.

Commonly carried out in large car parks or, less commonly, smooth grassy fields, autotests require the driver to manoeuvre his car through a series of obstacles marked out by cones (known as pylons). These obstacles vary from 'garages', to 'gates', to 'boxes', mixed in with reversing sections, slaloms and sudden direction changes; merely understanding the course diagrams given out at the beginning of each event is a daunting task, let alone memorizing it all.

A 'garage' is a rectangular area marked out by four cones, into which the competitor must drive – either forwards or in reverse – and then stop with all four wheels within the garage area; a box is a larger area within which the competitor must drive in a circle without hitting any of the marker cones; a gate is made up of two cones with a line between (either actual or imagined) astride which the car must stop.

The actual memorizing of each particular test leads to one of the most amusing aspects of the average autotest, as the drivers enact the whole course on foot. The sight of 20 or so very serious-looking people, all intently studying sheets of paper while negotiating a course of pylons, is quite hilarious, especially when they reach the reverse section and all flick round and commence walking backwards.

Autotesters utilize a number of specialized techniques, the most common being the handbrake turn and the reverse flick, both described in Chapter 7. The latter is really a handbrake turn but in reverse, and can be quite hazardous if not executed properly. Nevertheless it remains the quickest way by far of changing a car's direction from reverse to forwards. Or from reverse to upside-down if it is not executed with the driver on the inside of the turn....

Autotests are probably the easiest motor sport events to organize and to compete in, and as a result most RAC-affiliated motor clubs hold at least one

A deftly driven Mini stops precisely astride a 'gate'. The venue is a motorway service area car park

event every year, with an increase in popularity of the short evening autotest held during the week, where both drivers and newer organizers gain valuable experience in a relaxed atmosphere. In addition, the various Associations of Motor Clubs (Chapter 2) have their own championships. For those who want to take it all a bit more seriously, there is the BTRDA (British Trials and Rally Drivers Association) Autotest Championship, with 17 different awards including a Ladies' Trophy and special novice and non-expert award, and the RAC MSAs own British Autotest Championship.

The BTRDA Championship is broken down into seven separate classes:

Class A: Saloon Cars under 11 ft, up to 1100 cc;
Class B: Saloon cars under 11 ft, 1101 cc and over;
Class C: Saloon Cars from 11 ft and under 13 ft, any capacity;
Class D: Saloon Cars 13 ft and over, any capacity;

Above Chopped-top Minis are popular autotest vehicles, but don't make very good road transport unless weather protection is fitted

Below A Midget smokes its tyres away from a 'gate'. Speeds are low, but there is considerable wear on tyres and transmissions

Class E: Sports Cars;
Class F: Specials;
Class G: Junior Drivers (under 20).

To compete in an autotest your car must comply with the general requirements laid down in Section QA of the RAC MSA *Blue Book*, which relates to items such as fireproof bulkheads between driver and engine and engine and fuel tank; marking of battery earth leads; positively marked ignition switch, and so on. All fairly basic stuff that applies to all competition cars whatever their classification.

Other than those requirements there's not much else you would wish to do to the car. Tuning is a bit pointless, roll-cages are unnecessary, and the only thing worth doing if you're very serious about the whole thing is playing around with tyre sizes and pressures. Your only real expense other than tyres may be in transmissions, as sudden directional changes can take a toll on driveshafts and gearboxes, especially first and second gears. This is

Totally unmodified shopping cars can be used for autotests – one of the cheapest forms of motor sport

more of a problem on tarmac events; autotests carried out on grass are far less demanding on the car.

Licence required: Clubman C, Clubman RS, Speed or Rally.

Club membership required: Local motor club membership and/or BTRDA membership. BTRDA membership secretary: Liz Cox, 19a Oxford Street, Lambourne, Berks RG16 7XS. Tel: 0488 72027.

Further information: BTRDA Autotest Committee Secretary, Bernard Baker, 142 Highfield Road, Ipswich, Suffolk IP1 6DJ. Tel: 0473 41071.

BMW Challenge

We have BMW-enthusiasts Peter Brown and Jon Hooker to thank for proving that there are some BMW owners who know that there is more fun to be had from these yuppie totems than merely posing around outside wine bars. For it was Peter and Jon who got together with the BRSCC to formulate a racing series for owners of BMWs.

The BRSCC BMW Challenge is open to any production or production-based BMW models in roadgoing trim and possessing current MoT certificates where appropriate. In keeping with the principles of the Challenge, all cars must be driven to and from the circuits; trailering is prohibited. Despite the image of the BMW as a high-priced luxury product, some of the older and less fashionable models can be picked up very inexpensively, and given the minimal modifications allowed in the two Standard classes this could work out to be a very economical form of motor racing.

There are six classes:

Class A: Standard Production up to 2000 cc;
Class B: Standard Production 2000 to 2800 cc;
Class C: Standard Production over 2800 cc;
Class D: Roadgoing Modified up to 2000 cc;
Class E: Roadgoing Modified 2000 to 2800 cc;
Class F: Roadgoing Modified over 2800 cc.

Of these classes, A, B and C are the most restricted and will appeal to the competitor who wants to keep his car in as near to standard specification as possible. In all classes the cars must, of course, comply with the general RAC regulations relating to circuit racing cars, especially those which concern safety items such as roll-bars, fireproof bulkheads, extinguishers, full harness seatbelts, etc.

But other than those specifics the Standard classes allow only minor suspension modifications – free springs and dampers – and a frugal 1 in. extra on wheel rim widths. And apart from the removal of carpets and changing the seats for racing versions, that's all you can do.

For those with a lot more performance on their minds, the three Modified classes will no doubt have more appeal. The standard floorpan, sills, door surrounds, bulkheads and roof must remain standard in construction, dimension and material but the bodywork is virtually free, which means that fibreglass panels, perspex windows and so on

Above This is not the quickest way to drive a BMW, but it certainly pleases the spectators!

Below Older models can be picked up very cheaply, and are eligible for the BMW series. Look for a sound road car or a modified competition car like this 2002ti

are okay, along with gutted out interiors. However, the standard silhouette in side elevation must be retained so you can't build something that looks like a tall Group C car!

Engine modifications are unrestricted in the Modified classes except for dry sump lubrication, which is banned. Cars with forced induction – turbocharging or supercharging – will be subject to an equivalence factor of 1:1.4. Thus a turbocharged 2.3-litre will count as $2300\,cc \times 1.4 = 3220\,cc$, which will put it in Class F rather than Class E.

Suspension modifications are also largely unrestricted, the only proviso being that the original configuration is retained. Likewise transmission, which is free provided that the location and type for the model in question is not altered. Braking systems are also free.

Wheel diameter and type is free, but limited to a maximum rim width of 1 in. over the standard specification. As usual, tyres must be from the RAC List 1 for Production Racing Tyres.

Licence required: Restricted Race with medical certificate.

Club membership required: BRSCC, Brands Hatch Circuit, Fawkham, Dartford, Kent. Tel: 0474 874445.

Series co-ordinator: Chris Wadsley, BMW Car Club Motor Sport Division, Ridge Farm, Watlington, King's Lynn, Norfolk. Tel: 0553 810467.

Above left **Good preparation is the way to motor sport success, no matter how much money you have to spend. Many amateur-run cars can match the standards of preparation of this 'works' BMW**

Below left **Well-matched BMWs can provide good, close competition – this race was a round in the County BMW series**

Classic saloon racing

The Classic Saloon Car Club (CSCC) organizes two racing championships for those whose proclivities tend towards the roadgoing tin-tops of yesteryear: The Pre '57 Saloon Car Challenge and the Pre '65 Saloon Car Challenge. The great thing about these series is that they bring into the motor racing sphere a wide range of cars that are generally cheap to buy and which would otherwise be dismissed as old bangers. In keeping with the types of car involved, the aim of the club is to create a series of races which owe more to the principles of good fun rather than the (lack of) principles of win or bust.

Both of the championships take in around ten races, spread around most of the country's major racing circuits. The club has members coming from all parts of the country, and they range in experience from the complete novice to the seasoned driver, with 'late greats' like Sir John Whitmore dicing with lesser 'legends of their own housing estate'. Likewise the cars used range from the ultra cheapies in the Pre '57 Challenge to the lovingly cherished 'classic' saloon cars of the Pre '65 Challenge, although it has to be said that some '57 machines are not exactly starved of loot and affection, and may represent a greater investment than the less expensive elements of the other series.

Although both of the championships are controlled by age eligibility, a certain latitude is allowed, such that a 1966 Anglia, for example, would be permitted in the Pre '65 category as long as it was a model that was extant in 1965.

One novel – and potentially cost-cutting – aspect of the CSCC series is that team entries are allowed, with two or more drivers sharing the same car during the series; although none of the drivers will be likely to feature high in the individual championship (unless one driver does the lion's share of the driving) they can all score points towards the team championship. And it is obvious that if the costs are split two or three ways then the individual cost of competing is much reduced.

Pre '57 saloon cars These must be roadgoing saloon cars *marketed* before 31 December 1956, and as listed by the CSCC annually. All cars must comply with current Road Traffic Act, Motor Vehicles (Construction & Use) Regulations and Road Vehicle Lighting Regulations and must carry a

Variety is the name of the game in classic saloons, and you don't get much more variety than this

current D.o.E. test certificate which must be produced at pre-race scrutineering. The most popular machines seem to be Mk I, VII and VIII Jaguars, Ford Zephyrs, MG Magnettes, Morris Minors and Austin A35s, with the odd rarity such as the Borgward Isabella sneaking in among the Brits.

The cars break down into three capacity classes:

Class A: Over 1902 cc;
Class B: 1252 to 1901 cc;
Class C: Up to 1251 cc.

In outline all cars must comply with the RAC MSA Vehicle Regulations laid down for racing cars in Section Q of the *Blue Book* (see Chapter 2).

In addition the CSCC regulations are structured primarily to minimize modifications other than those that relate to safety, and to maintain the essential roadworthiness of the cars in order to achieve friendly and economical motor racing.

Thus lightening or reducing chassis strength is prohibited, whereas strengthening the chassis is recommended. Ground clearance must not be less than 4 inches for any part of the body/chassis excluding silencers and exhausts, and proper silencers must be fitted.

The bodywork must be complete, and standard in shape and material, and all external trim and bumpers must remain intact, likewise all internal bulkheads, sub-assemblies and chassis members – although they may be strengthened. However, where original materials are no longer available local repairs can be carried out using alternative material provided that the repair is of adequate strength.

If you want your car to look like a real racer you can strip out the interior trim and the heater just so long as the original dashboard and door trims remain, and you can fit as many additional instruments as your blood pressure can stand – there's a lot to be said for blissful ignorance sometimes! For safety reasons you can fit a non-standard seat and steering wheel, and as in all classes of racing I would recommend you opt for the kind of racing seat that provides an integral head restraint.

The CSCC regulations concerning engine modifications are quite liberal, but the engine block and cylinder head must be the original production items, and the engine must remain in the original position. Forced induction (turbocharging and supercharging) and fuel injection are only allowed if they are standard specification for the car, but carburettors can be replaced with those approved by the CSCC. Apart from a ban on dry sump systems, the rest of the engine is free from restrictions, and in addition cars with side-valve engines may fit ohv conversion kits – but only if the kit itself was marketed before 31 December 1956.

Like the engine the gearbox must remain in the original position (sounds obvious but don't underestimate the ingenuity of some motor racing characters!), otherwise anything goes apart from gearboxes or transaxles with rapidly interchangeable ratios – or, indeed, proprietory racing boxes. Axles again must remain in the original position and the casing must be original, although you can get away with a certain amount of 'local'

Spectators always love a good David and Goliath battle, and there are plenty of them in classic saloon racing

modification to allow the fitment of devices such as anti-tramp bars, Panhard rods, lowering blocks and suchlike. What you can't get away with is locked, torque-biased or limited-slip differentials unless fitted as original equipment.

Suspension type and spring type must remain the same as original, so no coil spring conversions are permitted. In fact, all original suspension components must be retained in their original positions as must all suspension pick-up points. Spherical bearings (Rose joints) may only be used if fitted as original equipment – so you are not likely to see many of *those* on a Pre '57 racer. The only real freedom applies to the additional suspension mentioned above and to dampers, which may be adjustable and/or uprated provided the standard type (i.e. lever, telescopic) is retained.

Finally – and significantly – quite stringent controls are placed on wheel specifications and size and types of tyres. Wheels must be made from steel, unless supplied otherwise as original equipment, and must be within 1 inch diameter of the original. Maximum wheel rim widths are laid down as follows:

Class A: 6.0 in.;
Class C: 5.0 in.;
Class D: 4.5 in.

The CSCC has its own list of eligible tyres, which nevertheless must not have an aspect ratio of less than 70 per cent.

Pre '65 saloon cars This is a wonderful championship for those who were spectating during the heyday of saloon car racing, when Jimmy Clark and Graham Hill performed automotive gymnastics in the Lotus Cortina, and the works' Mini Coopers, Imps and Anglias fought David and Goliath battles with the mighty V8 Galaxies and 3.8 Jaguars.

Eligible cars are roadgoing saloons marketed

Right It may look docile, but this particular A35 is a highly modified race car with Formula 3 specification engine, brakes and suspension

Below Big Jags have always been very popular among racing competitors – although these days they're becoming almost too valuable to race

before 1 January 1965 and listed by the CSCC annually. They include most cars of the type that were to be seen racing in the early 1960s, with the notable exclusion of Mini Coopers, which are deemed by the club to be far too highly developed these days, and also thoroughly well catered for in other classes of racing. The cars compete in five classes:

Class A: Over 3000 cc;
Class B: 2300 to 2999 cc;
Class C: 1200 to 2299 cc (except for those cars in
    Class E);
Class D: Up to 1199 cc;
Class E: Specified vehicles with engine capacities
    as Class C.

Broadly speaking, the regulations for Pre '65 cars are the same as for the older cars, but with a couple of fairly important differences. Limited-slip differential units are allowed, and maximum wheel rim widths are as follows:

Class A: 6.5 in.;
Class B: 6.0 in.;
Class C: 5.5 in.;
Class D: 5.0 in.;
Class E: 5.5 in.

While the Pre '65 series tends to be the more expensive of the two series there is a certain amount of overlap in terms of cost, with some of the Pre '57 competitors spending more on their cars than the cheaper end of the '65s. However, common to both is the closeness of the racing and the friendly atmosphere that permeates CSCC events. And while a high number of competitors choose to trailer their cars to events – especially in the more modern series – all the cars have to be road legal and many of them double up as their owner's day-to-day transport.

Licence required: Restricted Race with medical certificate.

Club membership required: The Classic Saloon Car Club GB, G. J. Masters, 69 Avalon Road, Ealing, London W13 0BR.

Drag racing

Drag racing. The very words bring to mind images of fire-breathing, nitro-burning Top Fuel dragsters or Funny Cars powered by mega-cube V8s. It isn't often that the same words make you think of a bog-stock Cortina trundling up the quarter mile, the driver white-knuckled and sweating as he urges his steed on past the Escort in the other lane. But there's no reason on earth why that Cortina – or your car! – shouldn't be there just as much as that Top Fueler. Drag racing is for everybody.

The requirements are few – a competition licence, crash helmet and adherence to certain rules regarding driver safety as laid down by the governing bodies. In the 'Production' classes, there is a requirement that your car be fully street-legal with only the most basic of modifications being allowed. In 'Street' you may modify the car much further but still there is a need to keep your car within the bounds of street drivability. 'Super Street' classes – as the name suggests – allow you to modify the car to a high degree, with street legality being stretched to the limit! The choice is yours – but best of all, it needn't cost you much to get started in this most American of motor sports.

In a nutshell, drag racing is all about covering a standing start quarter mile in the shortest time possible. The driver 'stages' his car (i.e., brings the vehicle to the startline stopping just short of triggering the timing beam) and awaits the countdown of the 'Christmas Tree' – the sequential start lights. On the green, it's a matter of going all out for the finish in an endeavour to cover the 440 yards in as short a space of time as possible. At the end of the strip is a second timing beam which, when broken, automatically stops the watches. The car that crosses the line first, wins. This 'Heads up' racing as it is called sounds nice and simple – and indeed it can be, as proven in the Super Street classes – but the drawback is that because the quickest car wins, the financial outlay necessary to build a winning car can be astronomical. This is where 'Index' racing comes to the fore.

In this type of drag racing, cars are handicapped with a delay built into the Christmas Tree starting lights, the length of which is dependent on the times recorded by the driver in practice. For example, you might record times of 14.6 seconds, 14.7 seconds and 14.5 seconds in your three practice runs. 'So',

Right Getting the rear tyres hot and sticky by spinning them in special traction compound

Left Virtually standard road cars can compete in 'Index' racing and 'Run what you brung' events

Below left Customized road cars with big engines and modified suspension make popular drag machines

Below A Cobra heats up its tyres prior to making a timed run

you might think, 'I can reckon on doing the quarter mile in 14.5 seconds if I try hard again!' Fair enough, but your first round opponent might have opted for (or 'dialled in') a time of 17.3 seconds. This will mean that the Christmas Tree will have a 2.8 second

delay programmed in favour of your opponent. You will have to sit there patiently for 2.8 seconds after the other guy has started – it sounds simple enough, but in the heat of the moment it is all too easy to start early and be disqualified for jumping the start ('drawing a red light' in drag racing parlance).

In theory you should both arrive at the finish at the same time, but rarely is this the case. You always try harder when there's competition in the air! The winner in this form of racing is the person who covers the quarter in the time closest to his dialled-in time or 'index'. If you go faster ('break out'), you lose. If you both break out, the one who does so by the smaller margin wins.

The ideas behind this form of racing are twofold; firstly, it builds up consistency by encouraging the driver to drive smoothly, time gearchanges to perfection and not 'save it all for the final'. Secondly, it enables any type of car to compete on equal terms with the mightiest muscle car – remember, it's consistency that counts.

But there is also another form of drag racing that you can take your road car along to – the 'Run What You Brung' or RWYB. This isn't strictly speaking racing in the sense that it doesn't require any form of competition licence, unlike the previous Heads up or Index races, but is seen to be unofficial practice. However, there's nothing to stop you from finding out on the strip who's got the fastest car in your street! All you need do is turn up, sign on and queue up for your turn down the quarter mile. Believe me, once you've sat on the startline and felt the adrenalin pump as the Christmas Tree starts its countdown, you'll be hooked.

Licence required: None for RWYB, Restricted Speed for other types.

Club membership:
Santa Pod Promotions, PO Box 196, Bromley, Kent BR2 0YS.

National Drag Racing Club, 154a Nelson Road, Whitton, Twickenham TW2 7BU.

British Drag Racing Association, c/o Yvonne Tramm, 29 West Drive, Caldecote, Cambs CB3 7NY. Tel: 0954 210028.

National Drag Racing Association, Mark Rumbold, 61 Chedworth Close, Church Hill, Redditch, Worcs. Tel: 0235 32402.

Hillclimbs and sprints

These two categories are covered together because of the great similarities between them and the types of car which compete. If you are unclear as to what precisely comprises a hillclimb and a sprint, refer to Chapter 1 of this book, where each type of motor sport is explained; suffice to say that hillclimbing has nothing to do with scaling muddy banks, and with a few exceptions sprints seldom involve blasting along in a straight line without a single corner to negotiate.

Despite the fact that between them they constitute one of the most popular forms of motor sport in the country, it is difficult to provide a precise breakdown of regulations as far as road-going classes are concerned. The RAC *Blue Book* lays down regulations for hillclimb and sprint cars competing in the major National championships, but as these championships seldom contain classes specifically for road cars the regulations are therefore not too relevant. However, virtually every motor club actively involved in motor sport has at least one hillclimb or sprint on its calendar; suffice to say that almost any type of road saloon or sportscar, provided it complies with the basic RAC Regulations (Section QA), will be eligible for an event somewhere. Contact your local motor club or Association of Motor Clubs to determine who is doing what in your area.

Most clubs seem to settle for the minimum RAC safety requirements for the roadgoing classes, which means that all you have to do is ensure that main bulkheads are fire- and fluidproof, paint the battery earth lead yellow, buy yourself a crash helmet, and away you go. Other clubs may require a bit more safety preparation, such as roll-over bar and full harness seatbelts . . . it all depends on the organizing club and the level of competitiveness of the event in question. At a more serious level, where timing is carried out by a light beam, cars will usually be required to fit a vertical strut mounted at the front of the vehicle to break the light beam; this must be opaque and non-reflective, measuring

Nic Mann's alarming and very fast sprint car was once a Morris Minor! It is still road legal

Above **This Dutton kit car combined with a Rover V8 engine makes a powerful combination for sprinting**

10 × 2 in. and mounted between 8 and 18 in. from the ground.

By far the best way to find out more about hillclimbs and sprints is to join the Hillclimb and Sprint Association. This was founded back in 1978 to bring together people interested in this type of sport and to further the aims of hillclimbing and sprinting around the country.

In March each year the Association holds a practice day at the Curborough Sprint venue near Lichfield, Staffordshire, where competitors can do some shakedown testing and newcomers can learn a bit more about the sport. This is an excellent way of finding out what other people are doing and the kind of cars that you are likely to come up against during the year.

In addition the Association has initiated a Beginners' and Novices' Sprint which is specially biased towards ordinary road cars, and in general there is a stronger leaning towards road car classes as

Left **This roadgoing Capri is competing at the famous Brighton Speed Trials, one of the oldest events in the sprint calendar**

Below **Sprinting is a relatively safe way to exploit the performance of your expensive exotic, though not everyone has a Ferrari to play with**

competition becomes more and more expensive.

The extremely enthusiastic MG Car Club organizes a combined Sprint and Hillclimb Championship which is open to any MGCC member using any make or model of MG, in roadgoing or modified trim. Points are awarded in classes so that the championship will be won by the most consistent driver, not necessarily the one with the most highly modified car. By far the highest proportion of cars competing in this popular series are the members' sole means of transport and 75 per cent of them drive their cars to the events. The venues are spread around the country from Wiscombe Hillclimb in Devon to Lydden Hill circuit in Kent and Ingliston circuit in Scotland, with five rounds counting towards championship points ... although the more rounds you can manage the better, because then you can count your five best results and drop the worst ones.

The regulations are quite liberal; apart from the basic RAC requirements most MGs are okay to run as they are, with the exception of Midgets and MGAs, both of which need some attention paid to making the rear bulkheads fireproof – an easy task, even for complete mechanical dunces.

Hillclimbs and sprints really are one of the most rewarding and inexpensive ways of getting into speed-biased tarmac motor sport, and with local events taking place all over the country there's no reason to spend a fortune on travel costs either. They also provide an excellent grounding in precision driving and car control for those who wish to move on into circuit racing at some stage.

Licence required: Clubman RS or Restricted Speed.

Club membership: Marcel Junod, Secretary, The Hillclimb & Sprint Association, 22 Silhill Hall Road, Solihull, W. Midlands B91 1JU.

MGCC Speed Championship, Jackie and Charlie Hayter, 49 Breach Avenue, Southbourne, Emsworth, Hants.

Above left **If you're important enough, who's going to complain if you use the company car for a spot of motor sport?**

Below left **A Bentley Turbo Mulsanne smokes its tyres away from the line at the Brighton Speed Trials**

Italian Inter-Marque Challenge

Lovers of all makes of Italian automobilia can now indulge their wildest fantasies thanks to the recent introduction of the Italian Inter-Marque Challenge. This is open to any production or production type car of Italian manufacture. Brands Hatch may not be the Mille Miglia and your Fiat 128 may not be a Maserati 250, but all race circuits have a challenge of their own and all Italian cars – no matter how humble their origins – seem to be permeated with that unique Latin *brio* and a fiery charisma.

The Challenge is aimed firmly at the club enthusiast and the emphasis is very much on keen amateurism rather than 'pot hunting' professionalism. Competitors come from all walks of life, but they are all bound together by an unswerving devotion for Italian motor cars, from the humblest Fiat up to the most exotic Ferrari.

There are no less than eight classes to choose from, four for Standard Production cars and four for Modified cars. The classes break down like this:

Standard Production	Modified	
Class A	Class E	Up to 1300 cc
Class B	Class F	1301 to 1600 cc
Class C	Class G	1601 to 2000 cc
Class D	Class H	Over 2000 cc

Italian cars seem to have an in-built sportiness as part of their character – they cry out to be raced

Inter-Marque racing is a good way to give your spare Ferrari an airing – but if the expense is a problem a Fiat 128 will provide almost as much fun

As far as the regulations are concerned the word 'Standard' means 'as originally produced by the vehicle manufacturer', and as you will discover if you read on the Standard Production class is blissfully free of opportunities to spend huge wads of money.

In general, cars in all classes must comply with RAC MSA minimal safety regulations covering rollcages, fireproof bulkheads, seat harnesses, fire extinguishers, electrical cutouts, etc., and must also comply with sections QA, QG and QL of the RAC *Blue Book* (see Chapter 2). Specific regulations then apply individually to Standard Production and Modified groups:

Standard Production Classes A to D must retain the overall chassis and bodywork specification as standard except where it is necessary to carry out modifications in order to comply with the specified RAC regulations, such as fitting a fireproof bulkhead, for example. However, interior trim and passenger seats may be removed and an alternative steering wheel may be fitted, but the fascia can only be altered if it is necessary to do so in order to fit a front braced roll-over cage. All cars must retain

a minimum ground clearance of 4 inches.

Engine tuning is strictly limited in this group, with a change of carburation being the only significant modification allowed. And even then, you have to retain the same type, size and number of chokes, and size of carburettor body so there's not a lot to spend your money on there. Other than that minor concession, the fitment of an oil cooler and transistorized ignition are about the limit of engine modification, which has to be good news for the enthusiastic amateur who doesn't want to spend a fortune on his car – or, indeed, alter the specification of what could well be an appreciating asset.

As you might guess from the regulations so far, transmissions must remain totally standard, as must the electrical system.

Suspension is comparatively free, and you can change dampers, springs and ride height just as long as the springs remain the same diameter as standard and the ride height doesn't compromise the ground clearance rule. So although you can't do much to make the car quicker in a straight line, you can nevertheless have a crack at making it swifter through the corners.

You can't do an awful lot to make it stop better though, because apart from changing the friction material and fitting race quality brake hoses you can't tamper with the anchors; fortunate, then, that most Italian jobs come with pretty effective brakes as standard.

While wheels of standard appearance are encouraged, it is nevertheless permissible to use any type and diameter; however, the width may only be increased by a maximum 1 inch and must fit within standard, unmodified wheelarches. Wheel spacers are not permitted.

Tyres must be as listed in the RAC MSA *Blue Book* under QP 3.1, List 1.

Modified Classes E to H, allow for much more in the way of tuning and modifications, and are aimed at the competitor with perhaps a bit more time and money at his disposal coupled with the desire to make his car more suited to circuit use both in terms of handling and straight-line performance.

In these classes the floorpan – apart from the boot floor – must remain as standard except when alterations are necessary to comply with RAC MSA safety requirements.

However, bodywork modifications are free except that the car must retain its standard silhouette above the axle centre line of the car, and spoilers and other aerodynamic devices are only permitted if fitted as standard. As wheels and tyres are unrestricted in the Modified classes wheelarch extensions are permitted, and must cover the wheels and tyres as specified in the *Blue Book*. Standard classes and the use of trailers to get to and from the circuits is much more common, especially those running on proper racing tyres.

Permitted engine modifications are unrestricted except that the engine type for the car model in question must remain unaltered (e.g. 105 series Alfa Romeos must use four-cylinder Twin Cams, Lancia Fulvias V4s and Alfasuds Flat 4s). Dry sump lubrication is allowed, and the alternator may be removed, a horsepower-saving practice which is quite common in out-and-out race cars but which severely limits a vehicle's usefulness as a road car!

Turbocharging or supercharging of modified cars is okay, but incurs an equivalence factor of 1:4 – in other words, a turbocharged 1300 will be considered as having a capacity of 5.2 litres, thus all blown cars must run in Class H.

Modifications to the suspension are likewise virtually unrestricted, except that the original suspension method must be retained; in other words,

integral coil spring/damper units (known as coil-overs) may be fitted to a car with torsion bar suspension, but the torsion bars must remain in standard specification and normal operation.

Transmission modifications are unrestricted except for the proviso that type and location remain unaltered, while brake systems are entirely free as long as they comply with the overall RAC MSA Technical Regulations.

As you will appreciate, these regulations permit quite radical mechanical and bodywork modifications which tend to result in some pretty wild cars in the Modified group; for this reason the roadability of these cars tends to be somewhat more limited than in the Standard classes and it is commonplace for such cars to be non-roadgoing and trailered to and from the circuits. A road legal car could, obviously, be used to compete in the Modified group but could not be expected to be wholly competitive alongside the more radical race cars.

Licence required: RAC Restricted Race with medical examination.

Series co-ordinator: Michael Lindsay, 97 High Street, Linton, Cambs CB1 6JT. Tel: 0223 891219 (office hours only).

Club membership required: BRSCC, Brands Hatch, Fawkham, Dartford, Kent. Tel: 0474 874445.

The Lancia Monte Carlo is fast and good-handling as standard, and is an ideal candidate for road and racing

Kit-car racing

One of the biggest success stories in club racing over the past few seasons has been the growth in kit-car racing, providing as it does close motor sport with the added advantage that the competitor can build his own car from scratch. And there's no better way of understanding how your car works than actually bolting it together in the first place.

It is also, of course, a relatively inexpensive way of getting on to the racetracks in a car that will happily double up as everyday transport.

One of the main attractions of kit-car racing – for the competitor and spectator alike – is the vast variety of cars that take part, ranging from the sleek low profile racer 'replicas' such as the Westfield (Lotus II) and Ultima (Lotus 23), through 'clubbie' two-seater sportscars like the Sylva Leader and Spyder Silverstone to traditionally styled vehicles like the NGTC or the huge, thundering Atlantis.

Although kit-car racing has attracted some top quality drivers and some high-buck machinery –

Above When you've gone to the trouble to build a car that looks like this, how can you not race it? Kit cars make excellent racers

Below Hi ho Sylva! A Sylva Striker hotly pursued by a Sylva Leader

An Aristocat and a Westfield II – both home-built kit cars – on the grid at Oulton Park

inevitable when on-track success can result in increased kit sales – the core of the sport remains resolutely in the domain of the keen amateur, the sort of person who has scraped together enough cash to build himself a nice but fairly humble kit car and has the inclination to take it on to the racetrack. After all, where better to prove how good an engineer you are than in competition with other like-minded individuals?

There is one two-part championship for kit cars, run by one of the country's leading motor sport clubs, the 750 Motor Club. The 750 MC series incorporates two separate championships run simultaneously, one for fairly extensively tuned cars and the other for budget kit cars.

750 Motor Club kit cars All cars for this series must be recognized roadgoing kit cars, excluding any cars already listed for the 750 MCs own Roadgoing Sportscars championship (see page 86). In practice this means that neither the Caterham Super Seven nor the Ginetta G15 – both of which are, or have been, available in kit form – is eligible.

All cars must be fully road legal and have valid road tax and MoT certificates which must be produced at signing on.

Classes are as follows:

Class A: Up to 1300 cc;
Class B: 1301 to 1600 cc;
Class C: 1601 cc and over;
Class D: Up to 1300 cc (Budget);
Class E: 1301 to 1600 cc (Budget);
Class F: 1601 cc and over (Budget).

Safety regulations and basic technical regulations are to RAC MSA requirements laid down in the *Blue Book*. Basically these require FIA specification roll-bars, full harness seatbelts, 1.5 kg capacity fire extinguisher, a rear warning light and an electrical cutout switch.

Engines must be based on series production units and may be tuned in any way so long as there are no more than two valves per cylinder and no turbocharging or supercharging is used on engines over 2000 cc.

Transmissions must also be from a series production car; ratios are free, but specialized competition transmissions such as Hewlands are not permitted.

In order to limit cost and retain a sensible road-going element, wheel rim widths are restricted to 6 in. for Classes A, B, D and E and 7 in. for C and F. Tyres must be as listed in the RAC MSA Technical Regulations QP 3.1 List 1, Tyres for Production Saloon and Sports Car Racing, and must have a minimum tread depth of 3 mm. This latter requirement is to discourage the practice of 'tyre shaving', in which a new tyre is shaved with a Surform or similar tool to reduce the tread depth to the barest minimum, giving an advantage on dry tracks. It is not unknown in some theoretically low-cost forms of racing for ultra-competitive teams to carry a set of brand new tyres with maximum tread for wet weather use and an entirely different set, shaved or worn right down to the road legal 1 mm tread depth, for dry weather use. Of course these shaved tyres are good for only one or two races before the 1 mm minimum is exceeded and another set has to be similarly shaved. Not only expensive, but also outside the spirit of most racing series that specify the use of road tyres.

Suspension and brakes are free provided that no brake balance valves or driver-adjustable anti-roll bar devices are fitted, and the lowest part of the car within the track of the vehicle must be capable of passing over a block 3 in. high with the race driver normally seated.

Engine and transmission must be fully enclosed by the bodywork and no adjustable aerodynamic devices are allowed.

The cockpit of the car seen in plan view must be symmetrical about the longitudinal axis of the car and must contain a minimum of two full-size seats, while the passenger area must provide as much space as the driver area. If a tonneau cover is fitted over the passenger area it must be removable and of soft flexible material.

Aerofoils are not permitted front or rear, but spoilers are allowed. An aerofoil is a device which creates aerodynamic downforce in its own right, whereas a spoiler diverts airflow to create an aero-dynamic advantage, i.e., it enables the car to cut through the air better.

The Budget section of the championship has the same capacity classes but the cars are more restricted in terms of tuning. This means that they are financially more accessible, but of course somewhat slower. Basically the Budget regulations are the same as the less restricted cars, except that no spherical rod end bearings (Rose joints) are allowed, twin-camshaft engines are banned and the engines must retain the standard manifolds and carburettor.

Licence required: Restricted Race with medical certificate.

Club membership: 750 Motor Club, c/o Dave Bradley, 16 Woodstock Road, Witney, Oxon OX8 6DT. Tel: 0993 2285.

Above right **The author racing his Sylva Star kit car**

Right **A Darrian and a Westfield II dispute the racing line**

Lotus/Caterham Seven racing

If ever a car was designed as a dual-purpose (or duel-purpose) road/race car then it was the Lotus Seven, now manufactured and marketed by Caterham Car Sales and re-named the Caterham Super Seven. Yet despite three decades as the stalwart of the club racing enthusiast, only comparatively recently has the Seven been privileged with a racing series all of its own.

Organized by the BRSCC and supported by Caterham Car Sales, this racing Series has been introduced to enable roadgoing Sevens to race competitively without detracting from the car's road-going capabilities. Which isn't saying a great deal considering that the Seven, even in its most mundane specification, is about the nearest thing you'll find to a roadgoing racing car.

The regulations for this series actually state that: '... all engines must have tractable road manners, e.g. shopping at Sainsbury's!' and the organizers reserve the right to drive any competitor's car to establish its roadworthiness, and to refuse the car an entry if it does not conform to the spirit of the regulations. A ruling of such an arbitrary nature leaves a little to be desired but nevertheless gets over the point quite forcefully that out-and-out racing cars are definitely frowned upon.

The Caterham/Lotus Seven Racing Series is open to Lotus Super Seven Series 1 to 4, 1957 to 1973, and Caterham Super Seven Series 3 and 4, 1973 to the present.

The series is divided into three classes, these being determined by the types of engine fitted to the individual cars. The trusty pushrod Ford 'Kent' engine is common to all three classes but in three different capacities and states of tune:

Class A This is the group for the 'quick' end of the range, with three engines specified:

1 Ford 'Kent', 1800 cc with 0.505 maximum valve lift (inlet and exhaust) and maximum carburettor choke size of 38 mm. Suggested camshafts are the Kent Cams 244 (with or without high ratio roller rockers) or the Kent 254, although the latter is a bit

---

Below **The De Dion Super Sprint version of the Caterham Seven features a semi-independent rear end and 1700 cc crossflow engine.** (**Photo:** *Cars & Car Conversions*)

Right **The Lotus BDR engine gives the little Seven a staggering power-weight ratio, and makes for a car that out-drags a Porsche Turbo**

wild and could create tractability (and therefore eligibility) problems.

2 Lotus Twin Cam, 1800 cc with 0.425 maximum valve lift (inlet and exhaust) and maximum carburettor choke size of 38 mm.

3 Cosworth BDR, 1700 cc with 0.340 maximum valve lift (inlet and exhaust), maximum inlet valve size of 1.22 in. and maximum exhaust valve size of 1.0 in., and maximum carburettor choke size of 38 mm. The suggested camshaft for this engine is the Cosworth BD3.

With all three engines the maximum carburettor size is twin 45 Weber or Dellorto.

Class B Two engines are specified for this middle class, which has proved to be very popular:

1 Ford 'Kent', 1700 cc with maximum valve lift of 0.440 (inlet and exhaust), and maximum carburettor choke size of 33 mm. The suggested camshaft is the Kent Cams 234.

2 Lotus Twin Cam, 1700 cc with maximum valve lift of 0.340 (inlet and exhaust) and maximum carburettor choke size of 33 mm. The suggested camshaft is the standard Big Valve twin-cam version.

In both cases the maximum carburettor size is twin 40 Weber or Dellorto.

Class C Two engines are specified for the smallest capacity class, which represents perhaps the least expensive way to compete in the series:

1 Ford 'Kent' ohv, 1630 cc with maximum valve lift of 0.350 (inlet and exhaust) and maximum carburettor choke size of 32 mm. Suggested camshafts are the Cosworth (or equivalent) A2 or the Ford GT version.

2 Ford CVH, 1600 cc with maximum valve lift of 0.240 (inlet and exhaust) and maximum carburettor choke size of 32 mm. Suggested camshaft for this engine is the standard item.

Specifically excluded from all classes are turbochargers and superchargers.

All cars must be fully road legal, complying with Construction & Use regulations, and must be road

The nearest thing to a four-wheeled motorcycle, the Caterham Super Seven is a sportscar in the finest British tradition. (Photo: *Cars & Car Conversions*)

taxed, insured and MoT'd; documentary evidence of these latter three requirements must be produced at each race meeting. Competing cars must fall in line with general technical regulations laid down by the RAC MSA, and must comply with safety measures listed by the RAC for production sportscar racing categories. This means that all cars must have an FIA specification roll-over bar; full harness seatbelts; a 1.5 kg minimum fire extinguisher; ignition cutout switch; flameproof rear bulkhead; suitable oil catch tanks to prevent leakage on to the track; and finally a separate external spring for each throttle spindle. Nothing too onerous there, just enough to make the car safe without totally destroying its credibility as a road car.

As far as chassis and bodywork modifications are concerned the standard production specification is to be used as a guideline, including the use of a standard full windscreen. You can't go hacking the body panels around, not even a few holes to provide extra cooling, thus the roadgoing looks of the car are preserved. However, interior trim may be removed and an alternative driver's seat is permitted.

Chassis layout must remain the same, and so must the location of all major components within the chassis. In other words you can't blithely shift the engine back a couple of inches to help the handling; someone will certainly notice and you'll be out on your ear.

Certain additional components can be added, though, the most significant being an oil tank – dry sumping is permitted – and oil coolers.

The suspension is also tightly controlled; double wishbone front ends and four link rear ends are definitely out, as are uprated dampers other than those specified by Caterham Cars as standard fittings. On the other hand, spring rates are unrestricted and you can fit either Caterham Cars' own specified negative camber competition wishbones or have the outboard upright pickups on the standard wishbones altered by 4 mm to achieve the same result.

Looking at the transmission part of the powertrain, only transmission types used in production Sevens are permitted, and straight-cut gearboxes are only allowed in Class A. However, limited-slip differentials may be fitted, and final drive ratios are free.

Brakes are almost totally unrestricted, except that brake balance valves are prohibited.

The only other regulation of any great significance is that wheels are limited to 6-inch maximum width and tyres must be as per RAC *Blue Book* regulations QP 3.1, List 1.

The points scoring system in the championship is really novel, in that points are awarded according not only to finishing position but also to how many cars in the same class you beat in the process. This works out as follows:

1st in class: 1 point per car beaten + 1 point
for winning, max. 10.
2nd in class: 1 point per car beaten, max 8.
3rd in class: 1 point per car beaten, max. 7 . . .

. . . and so on down to 1 point maximum for 9th place or lower. An extra point is awarded for fastest lap.

By organizing the points system in this way the championship can't be dominated by someone competing in a poorly supported class.

For many years the Seven has been legislated against in various sportscar racing categories for the simple reason that it is too competitive when compared to almost any other production sportscar of similar capacity. One can, of course, understand the legislators because no one wants to see an all-comers' racing series dominated by a single make of car, but on the other hand it has always seemed a bit unfair that the Seven should be victimized simply because it is too damned good. The obvious solution has been a long time coming, but at last there's a fair and well thought out series available for fans of Britain's favourite traditional sportscar. And as an added bonus the Seven is probably the only production road car whose value can actually be enhanced by a touch of racing history rather than depreciated.

Licence required: RAC Restricted Race with medical examination.

Series organizers: The BRSCC, Brands Hatch Circuit, Fawkham, Dartford, Kent DA3 8NH. Tel: 0474 874445.

Caterham Car Sales: Seven House, Town End, Caterham, Surrey CR3 5UG.

If ever a car was designed as a dual-purpose road/race car, it was the Lotus Seven

MG racing

The letters MG are virtually synonymous with club motor sport, and even though the combined efforts of the various manifestations of British Leyland have done everything they can over the last few years to emasculate the name, the true spirit of the marque still lives on under the devoted auspices of the MG Owners Club and the MG Car Club.

Both these organizations enjoy a friendly rivalry, each vying with the other for the reputation as *the* club for true enthusiasts. This rivalry no doubt works to the great benefit of the MG owner who wishes to go motor racing, as he is faced with a considerable variety of MG-based championships at his disposal; in many cases it is possible to prepare a car eligible to compete in races organized by either club.

The great thing about MGs, of course, is that they have always been thought of as 'sporting cars' and as such are crying out to be unleashed on the racetrack with little in the way of modifications. Some of them may be rather slow by modern standards but the sportscar versions tend to have a low centre of gravity, good weight distribution and firm suspension, all of which immediately tailors them to the racetrack.

Racing at club level is not limited solely to the now-defunct 'classic' representatives of the marque, because even MG Metros and MG Maestros are accepted in certain championships – in fact, as long as they have an MG badge they are acceptable. But it has to be said that the sportier versions do look the part, and even the humblest bog-standard Midget will turn heads in the local high street when it's in basic race trim. Which is more than you can say for a Maestro. Or an MG1300 saloon, for that matter. Having said that, the more mundane variations on the MG theme do provide for exceptionally low cost motor sport, especially in the Standard classes.

There's lots of good cheap fun to be had racing in the MGCC Sprite/Midget Challenge

BARC/MGOC racing championship

The MGOC runs a national championship admin-istered by the British Automobile Racing Club (BARC). All production MGs are eligible, from the brand spanking new to the old and venerable, with the following exceptions: MGB GT V8s, all EFi Saloons and all Turbo Saloons.

Standard Mk 1 Austin Healey Sprites are okay, as are later model Sprites in standard form. Standard Mk 1 Midgets may run up to 1275 cc engines.

Regardless of specification, all cars must be fitted with a roll-cage as defined in the RAC MSA Tech-nical Regulations Section QM1, and head restraint as defined in QM13. All competitors are strongly advised to fit a full roll-cage as per RAC *Blue Book* 1988. It is recommended that all cars carry a securely fitted fire extinguisher of a minimum 2.5 kg BCF, and a full harness seatbelt must also be fitted.

The Standard class, as the name implies, is open to anyone with a virtually standard roadgoing MG. It serves as a brilliant introduction to motor racing and at the same time provides lots of excitement and entertainment for the more seasoned com-petitor with a bit of experience behind him.

All cars in this category must be completely road legal, except that Road Tax and insurance are not insisted on if the car is trailered to the circuit.

There are general regulations relating to all cars within the category, plus individual model regu-lations dealing with specifics which relate to each

The MGA is a popular choice among historic car enthusiasts

A trio of 'Bs' competing in the MGOC racing series

eligible model and which are designed to operate as a kind of handicap system.

The general regulations insist on original bodywork with bumpers and interior trim intact, and with standard type suspension using the original pick-up points and the standard number of leafs in springs. Lowering blocks are not allowed, nor are non-original type suspension bushes. Adjustable dampers are allowed but they must be of the original type, ie. lever arm or telescopic.

Engines, broadly speaking, can have the internal parts balanced and you can fit electronic ignition, an electric fan, a baffled sump to prevent oil surge on corners, an oil cooler, different carburettor jets and needles, and a non-standard air filter. The maximum rebore permitted is +0.060 in. The actual engine specifications and detailed modifications allowed for 1275 and 1500 cc Midgets and 1798 cc MGBs are given in the MGOC regulations. These are very detailed and leave no question unanswered as to what may and may not be done to these engines. In simplistic terms, you can do quite a lot of not very much; for example, removing metal from the conrods in order to balance them, but without the weight of the rod dropping below a specified minimum.

Being an important safety feature, brakes can be modified by the use of competition linings and 1275 cc Midgets can use the brake parts from the 1500 cc Midget to provide a dual braking system. Brake backing plates may be removed or reshaped to aid cooling, and rear wheel cylinders may be changed. However, ventilated disc conversions are forbidden.

Close ratio gearboxes and limited-slip differentials are banned, and the final drive ratio must be as standard for the model of car.

Using these basic regulations as an outline, we can move on to the specific model regulations which detail changes from the basic requirements:

MGB Fibreglass front wings, bonnets and spoilers are permitted, and the MGB GT may use a fibreglass tailgate with perspex rear window. The engine must remain as described in the general regulations, except that the B GT may use a different exhaust manifold.

The gearbox must be standard, and the differential ratio must be 3.9:1. A $\frac{3}{4}$ in. front anti-roll bar may be fitted.

MGB GT V8 wheels are permitted on all models, but the maximum tyre size is 175/70 × 14 and 60-series tyres are not allowed.

MGC The regulations for the C are the same as for MGBs except that the maximum permitted tyre size goes up to 185 × 15, and you can fit 60-series tyres if you wish. On the other hand, the standard exhaust manifold must be retained in all cases and no fibreglass tailgates or perspex rear windows are allowed. The differential must be standard MGC, and the ratios must remain unaltered.

Midgets and Sprites Not a lot you can do here either, although fibreglass wings and bonnets can be fitted on all but the Mk I Sprite. Exhaust manifolds are free. Maximum front anti-roll bar thickness is 11/16 in.

The gearbox must remain standard, and the differential units are specified according to model: 1500 cc model – 3.9:1 or 3.7:1; 1098 cc or 1275 cc models 3.7:1, 3.9:1 or 4.2:1.

Maximum wheel rim width is $4\frac{1}{2}$ in., with 155/70 × 13 tyres.

Magnette Z and the Farina No fibreglass panels are allowed anywhere, but the engine is free from restrictions as long as the original style block and head are used and any rebore does not exceed 0.060 in. Carburettors are also free as is the transmission. Well, you've got to allow the old dears to keep up, haven't you?

A front anti-roll bar may be fitted provided it isn't thicker than $\frac{3}{4}$ in., and the maximum wheel rim width is 5 in. although there's no restriction on tyres other than they come from the RAC List 1.

MG 1300 Saloons Like the Farina, no fibreglass panels are allowed but inside the car you can remove the entire rear seat. Engine regulations are the same as for 1275 Midgets except that the camshaft is free and twin $1\frac{1}{2}$ in. SU carburettors may be fitted. The hydrolastic suspension can be modified by means of a shut-off valve to balance the pipes or by using different shock absorbers. Maximum permitted tyre size is 155/70 × 12.

Race your car and then drive it home afterwards – an MGB harries one of its smaller brethren at Donington Park

MGT and Y Series You would be surprised at how racy some of these older MGs can be, keeping pace with many of their more modern counterparts. This competitiveness is achieved by allowing quite a bit of freedom in the regulations, with no limit on

Above **MGB V8s are some of the more powerful contenders in the MGOC Championship**

Left **Classic MGAs battle it out on the track**

engine tuning other than bore size and a ban on supercharging. There is no restriction on the use of fibreglass panels, and transmission is free although the gearbox must use the original casing; what you stick inside it is no one's business but your own. Wheels mustn't be wider than 5 in., though, and brake servos and disc brake conversions are not allowed on the TA, TB and TC models.

MGA The wings may be changed for fibreglass, but otherwise no body modifications are permitted. The engine is free (within the overall regulations), and MGB cylinder heads may be used provided they comply with MGB regulations for Standard cars. Original type carburettors and standard camshaft must be retained.

The transmission must be standard, and the only permitted differential ratios are 4.3:1 or 4.4:1. A front anti-roll bar of a maximum $\frac{3}{4}$ in. thick is allowed, while tyres are limited to a maximum of 175/70 × 15.

The same rules apply to MGA Twin Cams except for the cylinder head, in which case the standard valve sizes must be retained.

MG Metro No modifications are permitted at all, except for the Special Tuning spoiler which may be fitted. MG Metro Turbos must race in the Modified class.

MG Maestro 1600 The only permitted modifications are the removal of the rear seat and gas flowing the cylinder head. Maximum tyre size is 185/60 × 14. Sounds like good news for the company car owner. . . .

MGCC championships

While the MGOC opts for one all-comers' championship the MGCC prefers a number of separate championships tailored specifically to the various MG models.

The MGCC MGA Register racing championship

This surprisingly well-supported championship is exclusively for MGA models, and as mentioned earlier cars conforming to these regulations are also eligible for the MGOC series. The MGA Register Championship is divided into three classes:

Class A: Standard MGA;
Class B: Modified MGA;
Class C: Twin Cam MGA.

For our purposes, however, we shall only be concerning ourselves with Class A, as the other two classes are better suited to well-modified racing cars than to dual-purpose road/race cars.

MGAs are, of course, highly collectable and therefore quite expensive to purchase, so even if the minimum amount is spent on modifying an MGA for racing it still won't qualify as one of the cheaper forms of club motor sport. Having said that, there are many people who own – or wish to own – an MGA and who feel that the best place to explore its handling and performance is on the racetrack.

Competitors are asked by the Register to adhere to the 'spirit' of MGA racing by trying to keep costs to a minimum and not participate in any action that might cause costs to rise.

Class A cars must be road legal in all aspects and have a valid MoT Certificate. The class is open to 1500, 1600, 1600 Mk II and De Luxe models, with an upper engine capacity limit of 1687 cc; this allows for the 1622 cc block with a +0.060 in. overbore. Unless specifically stated in the regulations the cars must remain in standard specification – in other words, if the regulations don't say you can, you can't.

Parts fitted as standard to later models may be fitted to earlier cars – for example a 1500 may be fitted with a 1622 cc engine and the later MGA disc brakes, although I would imagine that most owners of roadgoing cars would wish to keep the specification as original as possible.

Although the bodywork must remain of standard shape and appearance fibreglass wings, outer sills and front valance may be used provided, in the words of the MGCC, they are 'of neat and tidy appearance'. All other panels must remain standard and may not be removed. Aeroscreens of a pattern similar to the original factory option may be fitted to roadsters.

The driver's seat may be exchanged for a racing type seat, and although the passenger seat must be retained the seat squabs may be removed, as may all internal trim and carpets.

Although not compulsory, full harness seatbelts and a roll-over bar as per the RAC MSA safety regulations are recommended; frankly, anyone considering racing an open car without a roll-over bar needs to have his head examined. Which is probably not a very popular opinion among those who compete in historic racing cars, but in their case the seating position of the cars does not lend itself to fitting roll-over structures and the accepted rationale is that the drivers are safer being thrown from the cockpit in the event of an accident. An iffy argument in my opinion, but then I don't race historic racing cars.

Tonneau covers may be fitted, but must be of flexible material; no rigid, slipstream-cheating metal or grp covers are allowed. However, perspex side and rear windows may be fitted to coupés.

Floorboards must be a chip off the old block, i.e. timber plywood no less than 10 mm thick. Aluminium floors are not permitted under any circumstances.

Uprated dampers are permitted, but not adjustable ones, and they must be of the original pattern which means that telescopic dampers are forbidden. Likewise the road springs must be original pattern such that no part of the two main chassis tubes is less than $6\frac{1}{2}$ in. above ground level. An anti-roll bar no thicker than 5/8 in. may be fitted.

The regulations concerning wheels are rather unusual, in that the wheels from an entirely different make of car are recommended. Although standard pattern MG wheels – 4J × 15 – are allowed the MGA Register recommends that for safety reasons the pressed steel wheels from later models of the Saab 900 should be fitted, and the regulations even include a photo of the wheel in question so there's no confusion.

Tyres must be from the RAC MSA approved list, and sizes 5.60, 5.90, 155 or 165 are the only ones permitted.

So to the engines. Cylinder heads are limited to 1622 specifications with standard valve sizes (1,567 inlet, 1,348 exhaust); other MGA type heads may be machined to accept the 1622 size valves, and early MGB heads having the same valve sizes may also be used. Mean combustion chamber pressure must not exceed 180 psi, so no radical skimming please.

The only carburettors allowed are pairs of the following: $1\frac{1}{2}$ in. SUs type H4; HD4; HIF4; HS4. The original butterfly throttle must be retained and the carburettors may not be gas-flowed, although the air filters may be replaced by ram pipes.

Electronic systems are not allowed but a 'sports' coil may be fitted.

The camshaft profile must remain as standard, with maximum lift of 0.35 in.

The transmission must remain fairly standard, with no close ratio boxes or straight-cut gears. The only axle ratios allowed are 4.3:1 and 4.1:1, and even though the MGB standard diaphragm clutch may be installed in place of the MGA unit the MGB competition friction plate and cover plate are forbidden.

An alternator may be fitted instead of a dynamo, choice of cooling fan is free, a standard exhaust system must be fitted and the whole car must weigh at least 16.5 cwt.

MGCC Sprite/Midget Challenge One of the most popular racing series among club competitors, this particular championship is not too dissimilar from

The author track-testing an MGCC MGA road/racer

the MGOC class for Spridgets. The aim is to provide a low-cost formula for roadgoing MG Midgets and Austin Healey Sprites up to 1500 cc, and the regulations are designed to keep the Challenge well within the reach of the average amateur competitor. To this end, direct financial sponsorship is expressly forbidden and any advertising on the cars is limited to the appropriate Challenge decals plus two 55 sq. in. decals on either side of the car. So if you've managed to do a deal with the local accessory shop for discount spares or a free racing seat or whatever then you may carry the shop's decals on the car; but you can't negotiate a few grand of direct cash sponsorship and then emblazon the car with signwritten evidence of your persuasiveness.

There are no class divisions, so the earlier Spridgets would not be terribly competitive against their more recent variants were it not for the fact that it is permitted to transplant later A-series engines into older chassis. But not the more recent 1500 cc Triumph engine, presumably because the bigger Triumph engine combined with the more nimble 1275 cc chassis would prove to be an invincible combination and thus reduce the flexibility of the Challenge.

The usual safety requirements are mandatory in all cars, in particular the use of a laminated glass windscreen, roll-over cage, full harness seatbelts, fireproof bulkheads, external electrical cutout switch and a 2.5 kg BCF fire extinguisher.

Although the basic steel monocoque of the car must remain unsullied, the MGCC do allow the front wings, bonnet, valence and boot lid to be replaced with fibreglass or aluminium alternatives, but streamlined bonnets, aerofoils, wings etc. are all prohibited to keep the cars looking as original and standard as possible. Carpeting and interior trim may be removed, but the passenger seat must be retained, although both seats may be swapped for matching racing versions if required.

The engine regulations are quite restricted. Balancing of internal components such as crankshaft, rods and flywheel are allowed, as is gas flowing of cylinder heads, but standard sized valves must be retained and in the case of the 12G 940 type cylinder head no modifications are permitted at all. Camshafts for the A-series engines may be either the AEG 577/323/538 or the C-AEA 800/731, but the Triumph 1500 engine must retain the standard camshaft.

Carburettors must be the original 1.25 in. SUs for the A-series, or the original 1.5 in. SUs for the Triumph engine, and exhaust systems are free as long as they remain road legal.

Moving on to suspension, you will find no more extensive modifications than you would expect on an averagely modified road car, i.e. lowered springs, uprated dampers, negative camber front trunnions and an anti-roll bar; telescopic damper conversions are allowed at the rear only.

As you would expect from a formula of this nature, transmission systems must remain more or less as standard, although differential ratios may be changed provided only other BL units are used. As for brakes, a servo may be installed and competition linings can be fitted but otherwise they must remain standard.

The road wheels must be standard steel pressing or original specification wires, and tyres must be ordinary road tyres up to a maximum 165 section and with a profile not lower than 70 series.

As a final control there are minimum weights listed, and any ballast required to achieve these weights must be fitted under the seats.

MGCC BC V8 championship This championship is divided into four classes:

Class A: Standard MGB & MGC;
Class B: Road Modified MGB, MGC and Standard MGB GT V8;
Class C: Full Race MGB and MGC;
Class D: Full Race MG V8.

As you will appreciate, it is the first two classes that interest us here.

Certain general regulations apply in both cases, covering the safety aspects of the sport. Full harness seatbelts, roll-cages, laminated screens, 2.5 kg extinguishers, battery cutout switches and fireproof bulkheads are all compulsory. Full details of specifications can, of course, be found in the RAC Year Book Technical Regulations (the *Blue Book* that is referred to constantly in these chapters).

Class A: This is intended for cars that are as close as possible to showroom specification, albeit with certain modifications to make them a little more raceworthy.

Accepting that steel front wings do tend to suffer from rot, the MGCC permit the use of fibreglass alternatives although they are not encouraged. One-piece grp front sections are certainly not allowed, however. Sebring-type headlamp covers are permitted, but the only acceptable aerodynamic aids are standard British Leyland Special Tuning pattern front and rear spoilers.

All fixed interior trim must remain in place but carpets and sill mats may be removed, and the seats may be changed for upholstered competition versions.

The engines must be standard production items but parts may be swapped around from earlier or later models. The only permitted modifications are: balancing of rotating parts; free carburettor needles; electronic ignition; removal of engine fan and fitment of electric fan; removal of the centre section of the exhaust system, to be replaced by a piece of pipe; replacement of the thermostat with a blanking sleeve; removal of the air filter, or replacement with pancake-type filters; a minimum combustion chamber capacity of 36 cc (MGB only). In addition, a 60 thou overbore is allowed, and the top face of the MGB block may be faced provided the pistons remain a minimum 0.010 in. down the bore on all cylinders.

Uprated or competition dampers are allowed, but unlike the Sprite/Midget Challenge rear telescopic conversions are forbidden. The 0.75 in. competition anti-roll bar and V8-pattern lower arm bushes are permitted, but not the use of Nylotron bushes anywhere in the suspension system.

The use of competition brake pads and linings is positively encouraged, and the rear brake cylinders may be replaced by Mini Cooper versions. Front brake dust shields may be removed, but otherwise the braking system must remain standard.

Competition clutches are the only permitted transmission modification permitted in the regulations.

Wheels may not be wider than 5 in., and should be either pressed steel or MGB GT or V8 alloy versions; they must be fitted with tyres from the RAC List 1 (see the *Blue Book*) no wider than 185 section and no less than 70 series aspect ratio.

Class B: The regulations for this class are somewhat more liberal but nevertheless provide for roadgoing cars that can still feasibly function as everyday transport, especially if you're the kind of person who likes to commute in something a shade more extrovert than normal.

One-piece grp front ends are still not allowed, but fibreglass or alloy door skins are okay, perspex windows are allowed (except for the front screen which must be laminated glass), while interior trim and passenger seats may be removed.

Permitted engine modifications are fairly free, but MGCs are restricted to a maximum overbore of 60 thou and MGBs to a maximum capacity of 1950 cc. The engine stroke must not be altered, and forced induction is banned, but carburettors and

A full grid of MGAs shows just how popular these venerable sportscars still are

exhaust systems are free as long as the car remains road legal.

All front suspension components except springs, dampers and anti-roll bars must be production items, but they may be modified. Fabricated components, rod ends and spherical bearings are only permitted in the anti-roll bar linkages.

At the rear of the car the standard axle casing must be used and rear springs must be the leaf type, but any form of axle location may be used, rod ends and spherical bearings are free and rear anti-roll bars are permitted.

The brake regulations are the same as for the Standard class except that MGBs may use GT V8 front discs and calipers; the MGC must retain its standard setup front and rear.

Limited-slip or locked differentials are not allowed, but close ratio gears are permitted provided they are installed in standard MGB or MGC casings.

Maximum wheel widths are 6 in. for MGBs and 7 in. for MGCs, and tyres are restricted to a minimum aspect ratio of 60 series and maximum section of 195. They must, of course, be standard road tyres.

The Standard V8 section of Class B only permits genuine factory-produced MGB GT V8s, but because of the short supply of original engines equivalent Rover units produced up to 1985 are permitted. Regulations are more or less as for Class A, but 6 in. wide wheels and 195/60 tyres are allowed.

Licence required: Restricted Race with medical certificate.

Club membership: MGOC Racing Team, MG Owners Club, 2/4 Station Road, Swavesey, Cambridge. Tel: 0954 31125.

MGCC MGA Register, joint competition secretaries: Mark Dollimore, 17 Alverton, Great Linford, Milton Keynes, MK14 5EF. Tel: 0908 605454 (H), 0908 612777 (B), Steve Smith, 9 Vienne Close, Duston, Northampton, NN5 6HE. Tel: 0604 585840 (H), 0933 227963 (B).

Sprite/Midget Challenge, competition secretary: Larry Quinn, 1 Dalwood, Thorpe Bay, Essex. Tel: 0702 582560.

BCV8 Championship, competition secretary: Peter Blackbourn, 16 Asylum Road, Peckham, London SE15. Tel: 01 639 2860.

Porsche racing

At last, a motor racing series for city slickers!

All right, I admit that's a bit unfair; in fact this Pirelli-sponsored series is thankfully free of the 'okay yah' brigade and is mostly made up of a varied mix of Porsche enthusiasts – the sort who actually know how to drive their 'Porkers' rather than just pose around in them.

The essentially roadgoing nature of the series is maintained by a novel means of policing the cars, plus a spirit of the regulations clause designed to ensure that no driver shall attempt to 'loophole' the regulations in order to run a car which does not fit in with the Porsche Club GB's definitions of a roadgoing Porsche.

All cars must comply fully with requirements for road cars, and must have valid road tax and MoT test certificates.

Unique among motor sport championships the Porsches are divided into classes according to their power output rather than engine capacity. These classes are:

Class A: Cars exceeding 208 bhp;

Class B: Cars exceeding 178 bhp but not exceeding 208 bhp;

Class C: Cars exceeding 140 bhp but not exceeding 178 bhp;

Class D: Cars not exceeding 140 bhp.

Additionally, all cars are subject to a minimum weight limit as listed for each model by the Porsche Club GB.

The power output classification is based primarily on the manufacturer's stated bhp for the given model, but the Porsche Club GB reserves the right to down-classify if appropriate any cars driven by competitors in their first year of competition. In other words, they may re-classify certain car/driver combinations in order to make them more competitive.

They will also permit a 5 per cent margin on bhp figures if they think it is justified.

All cars must comply with the RAC MSA Technical Regulations QA (All Vehicles) and QG (Race Vehicles) with a few exceptions which are listed in the detailed regulations.

The QG section requires only that open cars must have roll-cages, leaving it to the individual championship regulations to make them mandatory. In this case the PC GB strongly recommends roll-cages in all cars, along with proper fire-resistant overalls. Full harness seatbelts must be fitted, as must RAC approved fire extinguishers of a minimum 1.5 kg capacity.

Bodywork must remain standard except that grp front wings and bonnets may be fitted if they comply to the original shape; 1973 RS Carreras may fit grp rear bumpers to RS lightweight pattern. You are also allowed air scoops within certain limitations, and the battery and washer bottle may be repositioned – presumably to a more beneficial location, weight-wise.

Wheels must comply with the original specification for the car, but rim widths may be up to 7 in., except for cars with 7 J rims as standard which

Close racing? These two Porsches seem to be getting very chummy

Right Racing Porsches looks expensive – and some are – but these exotics need not cost a fortune if you shop around and know what you're looking for

Below One of the most desirable of all sportscars, the 911 Carrera – and it looks great in the pub car park as well!

Below right Paul Edwards powers his 'Porker' out of the hairpin at Mallory Park

are allowed to go up to 8 in., 3.3 Turbos and 928S models must be fitted with 16 in. diameter wheels, and on 911 models 14 in. diameter wheels may only be used in conjunction with self-levelling struts. Tyres must be road tyres as listed in the RAC MSA List 1, and shall be DoT marked. Special compounds are not allowed.

Standard spoilers only may be fitted, but you are allowed a certain amount of interchangeability between models.

The suspension must be standard except for reinforcement of the rear trailing arms on pre-'69 cars, but shock absorbers, springs and torsion bars are free as long as they remain of the standard type, and no additional springs sneak in. Any production Porsche anti-roll bar may be used provided it can be installed without modification and without the use of adjustable links.

Brakes, again, must remain basically standard but modifications to aid cooling are allowed within certain limits, and fluid and linings are free.

Right Porsches, Porsches everywhere, and a bit of paint-swapping among the Stuttgart supercars

Below Close action among the Porsches, while a few other makes look on in wonder

Below right Bill Taylor – one of the most successful of the Porsche 911 brigade in recent years

Bill Taylor braking hard for Druids Bend at Brands Hatch

The interior may be modified subject to the minimum weight requirements listed for each car by the Porsche Club GB, Carrera RS lightweight trim is allowed in the 1973 RS Carrera, and in all cases the driver's seat may be replaced by a suitably fixed racing seat. Remaining passenger seats may be changed, but must remain suitable for normal road use. Floor well carpets and hinged rear seat backs may be removed, and in the 924 the boot area carpet may be replaced by lightweight trim. The steering wheel may be changed.

So to the engines. These must be to standard UK specification for each model in question, with standard turbo boost where applicable and standard exhaust/silencer systems. They are, of course, subject to the listed power outputs permitted for each class.

The Porsche Club GB are totally committed to controlling the regulations for their championship and as such are prepared to check cars at random throughout the season to ensure their compliance with the regulations. To this end any registered competitor must accept that the organizers may remove his car for a period of up to five days, in order that full eligibility checks may be carried out. If this situation arises, the organizers will supply the competitor with a suitable replacement car free of rental for the period that his own car is impounded. Which seems like a remarkably effective way of ensuring that competitors toe the line.

Although Porsche Turbos and the like are not the cheapest cars around, some of the older or less exotic models can be picked up relatively cheaply and can provide a means of competing in this highly competitive and rather exotic championship. Just because the car is Porsche doesn't mean it's not affordable.

Licence required: Restricted Race with medical certificate.

Series organizer: J. F. May, Porsche Club GB, Doric House, 56 Alcester Road, Studley, War. B80 7LG. Tel: 052785 4108.

Club membership required: Porsche Club GB Motor Sport Division.

Production car trials

A wonderfully inexpensive form of motor sport that requires very low initial investment, minimal running costs, and the likelihood of exceptionally low maintenance and repair costs. What's more, it requires little in the way of bravery, is safer than trying to manœuvre a shopping trolley round Safeway's, and you can take a chum along to join in the action. In fact, a passenger is obligatory.

A production car trial, in simple terms, involves driving a car uphill along a number of different courses – known as sections – marked out by pairs of stakes. The aim is to get as far as possible along the section without going outside the stakes, hitting one of them or coming to a standstill. Penalty points are awarded for each misdemeanour (after which the attempt at the section ceases), and the competitor with the least number of penalties at the end of the day is the winner.

Sounds like a piece of cake, doesn't it? Which it would be, except the sections are invariably on the slipperiest surfaces possible – anything from mud, through wet chalk, to grass; are twisting and tortuous to the extreme; and more often than not include interesting natural obstacles like large rocks, trees, roots, potholes, and similar delights to be avoided at all costs.

With all its weight over the rear wheels the VW Beetle makes an excellent trialler

Traction is the name of the PCT game, which is why you carry a willing accomplice along to add his (or her) weight to provide extra grip. This must surely be the only form of motor sport where it sometimes helps to have a fat friend.

Like many other forms of motor sport PCTs are divided into classes so that like may be matched against like, and no one can be said to have an unfair advantage. The classes are:

Class A: Front-wheel-drive production cars up to 165.9 in. overall length and up to 1200 cc (except BL Mini, Hornet and Elf);

Class B: Front-wheel-drive production cars up to 165.9 in. overall length of over 1200 cc and BL Mini, Hornet and Elf;

Class C: Front engine and gearbox production saloon and convertible cars of 166 in. overall length and over (fwd and rwd) (except vehicles in Class F);

Class D: Front engine rear-wheel-drive production cars not eligible for Class C (except vehicles in Class F);

Class E: Rear engine production cars (except vehicles in Class F);

Class F: The following production cars: Chrysler Imp engine cars over 925 cc; Clan; Dellow; Davrian; Denzel; Frazer-Nash; Ginetta; Lotus 7; Panther Lima (except with 3.46:1 diff.); Dutton Phaeton (to approved specification). Plus other production cars manufactured on a limited basis and approved by the RAC MSA; cars fitted with torque biasing differentials as catalogued for that car; and cars not already listed in this class, modified to the RAC specifications for Classic Reliability Trial Vehicles.

Below **Some of the most unlikely cars get pressed into service for production car trials**

Right **The way we were – a helping hand for an old timer**

Class G: Four-wheel-drive vehicles sold in the UK through dealer networks, on which car tax is levied. The vehicles must be locked in high ratio.

That must surely be the most complicated class structure of any motor sport category, but it has been arrived at through experience and is designed to ensure that all cars competing against each other are as evenly matched as possible; furthermore, it enables an index of performance to be calculated and overall positions determined for the event.

Like all competition cars, those competing in PCTs must comply with the provisions laid down in section QA of the RAC MSA Technical Regulations, covering such things as fireproof bulkheads and so on. You won't need a crash helmet or expensive fire-resistant overalls, nor will you have to fit a roll-over bar or anything other than conventional lap and diagonal seatbelts.

As far as bodywork is concerned, it's 'hands off' if you want to get through pre-event scrutineering. Except you are allowed to remove bodywork ahead of and below the centre line of the front wheels to give a more advantageous approach angle, external mirrors may be removed, and you can fit a sump guard if you want. But bumpers must not be removed.

The addition of ballast is permitted, provided it is firmly secured within the bumpers or bodyshell and can't be shifted during the event. Also it mustn't protrude or be in any way visible.

Engine tuning is permitted, but you have to retain the original cylinder head and block. And unless in Class D, E or F, the carburettor(s) and manifolds must also remain as standard. Crankshaft stroke cannot be altered in any class, but a cylinder rebore of a maximum $+0.060$ in. is allowed.

There is another type of trials – known as Sporting Cars Trials – in which one of the more delightful features of the cars is the use of fiddle brakes which enable individual rear wheels to be locked up separately. This is an entirely academic point because you can't fit them to PCT cars, although you are allowed to increase braking power. You are also permitted to change the shockers – as long as the

Well-known motor sport photographer Chris Harvey, who provided many of the photos for this book, supplies the ballast in this Morgan. A hefty passenger can be a boon when the going gets slippery

mounting points remain the same – and fit anti-roll bars and anti-tramp bars if you wish.

Wheels must remain as the standard type fitted to the car, and tyres must be as listed by the RAC MSA for Production Cars, with the exception of certain high performance and all weather tyres which are not allowed. They must also be fitted in the size specified as standard by the car manufacturer for that model of car. However, ground clearance and tyre 'footprint' area are significant factors in PCTs and in cases where a modern car is fitted with low aspect ratio tyres it is permitted to change the aspect ratio one stage higher, provided that the width of the tyre is decreased by 20 mm. Thus a 205/60 may be replaced by a 185/70, and so on.

On certain surfaces low tyre pressures can be quite an advantage, but to stop things getting too silly tyre pressures on the driven wheels must not be less than the following:

Classes A, B* and C (plus Class F – fwd): 15 psi;
Classes D, E and F: 18 psi;
Class G (non fwd): 21 psi.
(* BL Mini, Hornet and Elf of 1100 cc and over are permitted 18 psi).

The great thing about PCTs is that you can compete in virtually any type of everyday car without too much risk of not being able to go to work in it the next day. And despite a certain amount of modification permitted within the regulations the majority of people compete in virtually standard cars.

Naturally some cars are better suited to the game than others, particularly those with the engine over the driven wheels, but the classes are structured to keep everything as fair as possible and whether you compete in a Porsche 911 or a Mk II Escort success is generally down to the driver (and his bouncing companion) rather than to the car itself.

Licence required: Club Card, Clubman C or RS, Rally.

Club membership: Local motor club and/or The BTRDA, membership secretary: Liz Cox, 19a Oxford Street, Lambourne, Berks RG16 7XS. Tel: 0488 72027.

Further information: The BTRDA Production Car Trials secretary, Sue Ludford, 27 Sherringham Drive, Essington, Wolverhampton WV11 2EB.

Road rallying

Rallying is arguably the single most popular form of motor sport in the country, and road rallying at one level or another is pursued by a large number of motor clubs throughout the country. Its main advantage is that the cars require little in the way of modification (although certain basic chassis preparation is desirable and more extensive tuning will be necessary if you want to be at all competitive); its main disadvantage is that road rallying generally takes place at night – right through the night – which can be rather anti–social, not to mention exhausting.

Road rallies tend to have a strong navigational element, therefore a good navigator is an important requirement. Events are lost and won on the ability of the crew to find their way to a number of checkpoints ('controls') which may be either a waypoint, i.e. you simply have to pass through it, or a time control, through which you must pass within a specified time.

The routes between controls are known as 'sections'. Competitive sections are those where a time penalty is imposed for late arrival or early arrival; non-competitive sections are those in which there is no individual time requirement, although competitors may be penalized for early arrival at controls or for missing them. There is also usually a Maximum Lateness allowance on most road rallies, and if you exceed that you are out of the event.

Competitive sections must not include any road with a 30 or 40 mph speed restriction; nor cross any A-road; they must not use more than 200 metres of any A-road; and must not require competitors to exceed an average of 30 mph.

Non-competitive sections must not be timed to an accuracy of less than 1 minute; they must not require an average of greater than 28 mph except on A-, B- or M-roads; they must be completed without the use of auxiliary lights; and must not be used to make up time lost on competitive sections.

Above right **Rallying is such a nice way to see the countryside – or to wash the car**

Below right **Want to know what to do on a wet weekend? How about a bit of rallying?**

Although the organizers will have informed competitors well in advance of the Ordnance Survey maps that will be required for each event, details of the rally route are not usually available until just before the start of the event, which really puts the navigator on trial. Sometimes little tricks are used by the organizers to make things even more difficult, such as defining a route by a series of problems rather than by straightforward instructions. For example, part of the route instructions may direct the navigator to go from one specified point to another without using A-roads, or without passing through a particular location, or without going over any crossroads, or fords, or level-crossings. Some sadistic organizers have even been known to provide the whole route on separate tracing paper overlays – with no instruction as to which part of the map those overlays apply.

As you will appreciate, in road rallying the navigator is at least as important as the driver. His role not only involves basic navigation from one point to another, but time calculations and route instructions to his driver.

The navigator's two main aids – apart from his maps – are a 'Roamer' and a Tripmeter. A Roamer is a simple plastic device used for plotting map references. Every Ordnance Survey map used for rallying is marked out in horizontal and vertical lines scaled 1 kilometre apart so that they form a grid of 1 kilometre squares all over the map. Each of these lines has a reference number, shown along the top, bottom and side edges of the map. Thus the corners of the squares can be plotted by simply quoting the numbers of the two intersecting lines at the point in question, e.g. a reference 2072 would refer to the point at which line 20 intersected with line 72. It is important to remember that references to vertical lines are always given before references to horizontal lines.

But in rallying you need greater accuracy than the corners of 1 kilometre squares, so you have to imagine each line divided up into tenths of a kilometre. Thus a reference given as 205725 (i.e. 20.5 and 72.5) would define a point smack in the middle of the square formed by lines 20 and 72. To complete the reference the map number is given first, e.g. 176/205725 means that the map reference applies to map 176. The reference is, in fact, somewhere in the middle of Richmond Park if you're interested. A Roamer is a transparent plastic square, worn on a lanyard round the neck, which

You don't have to invest a fortune in a brand new car to take up rallying

has printed on it a single kilometre square subdivided into tenths. It is simply used to measure off the tenths on the navigator's 1:50,000 scale Ordnance Survey map in order to plot map references.

A Tripmeter is really a sophisticated version of an odometer – i.e. a mileage or kilometre counter – and is used to measure the distance a car has travelled, or to count down to a pre-set distance. By using the Tripmeter a navigator can accurately assess distances travelled, and calculate average speeds. He can tell precisely where he is on the map, and provide the driver with a countdown to corners, intersections, controls, etc.

Armed with the right map, a Roamer and a Tripmeter any navigator worth his salt should be able to take you anywhere. And arrive there at the correct time.

Road rally cars must, of course, comply with Section QA of the RAC MSA Technical Regulations. In addition they must comply with all the appropriate regulations that relate to roadgoing cars, and must be taxed, tested and insured for the road. All cars must carry a red warning triangle for use in emergencies.

The bodywork must be as the manufacturer's original shape and profile, but may include any optional extras available directly from the manufacturer; wheelarch extensions can only be used if they are fitted by the manufacturer as a standard item for that body type.

Engines are restricted to a maximum of four cylinders, a maximum of two valves per cylinder, a maximum of two carburettor chokes and a maximum of one camshaft per bank of cylinders. Fuel injection is only permitted if fitted as standard, and forced induction isn't allowed at all. Twin Wankel (rotor) engines are not allowed. All cars must be fitted with an external spring to each throttle spindle such that the throttles will be closed in the event of linkage failure, and if a different engine is fitted it must not represent a capacity increase of greater than 50 per cent unless the conversion is inspected and approved by an official Group 1 or Group 2 RAC scrutineer. Which sounds like a safe and sensible attitude given that these cars are competing on public highways.

Wheels and tyres are quite tightly controlled, with a 6-inch rim width maximum and tyres limited to a maximum 185 section and no less than 60 per cent aspect ratio. Furthermore, the tyres must carry

either an E-rating mark or, in the case of remoulds, an S-mark or RMA marking.

An essential requirement for any car which competes at night must be a decent set of driving lights. However, the RAC regulations don't allow you to have more than four forward-facing lamps (excluding sidelights and indicators) and they must comply with road usage regulations in terms of wattage and operation. Any decent motor accessory shop will be able to supply you with a brace of auxiliary lights that are ideal for your needs. At the same time as fitting them you may as well install a map reading light for the man in the passenger seat, and possibly an external light over the passenger door to illuminate the activities of your navigator as he tries to convince the time control marshals that

Closed military ranges make ideal venues for club rallying. This is Epynt in Wales

you're not actually running ten minutes late!

Roll-cages and full harness seatbelts are not demanded by the regulations but most people like to install a decent pair of competition seats, preferably with built-in head restraints. Crash helmets are not required for road rallies and intercom systems are not permitted.

As far as tweaking up the car goes, you can do as much as you like provided you stay within the regulations. Some people run with completely standard engines, others like to extract a bit more power. The best bet is to try a couple of events and see how you get on; if you feel your car is hopelessly down on power then this is the time to consider some engine modifications. Really it all depends on the level of competition at your local events.

However, most people would be well advised to uprate the suspension a little if the basic car is rather mundane, with perhaps a decent set of gas-filled adjustable dampers. Sporty versions of some cars may already be fitted with suitably beefy suspension, and again it all comes down to how competitive you want to be and how much you're prepared to spend in achieving it. Certainly you can compete in road rallies at a very cheap level, altering the car very little from standard specification, particularly if you start off competing in '12 Car Rallies' which are events restricted to members of the organizing club and which have no more than 12 entries. These events require no special RAC permit to be taken out by the organizing club and as such demand no competition licence.

Licence required: Driver: Club Card, Clubman C or RS, or Rally. Navigator: Club Card, Clubman C or RS, Rally, or Navigator.

Club membership required: Local car club and/or The BTRDA, membership secretary: Liz Cox, 19a Oxford Street, Lambourne, Berks RG16 7XS. Tel: 0488 72027.

Further information: The BTRDA Rally, committee secretary, Rodger MacFarlane, Navidale, Blainslie, Galashiels, Selkirkshire.

Even old stagers make popular rally cars. Here a 'works' Healey 3000 competes on the Coronation Rally for historic rally cars

Road saloons

Just the thing for Jack the Lads with hot saloons in their driveway and the urge for trying their hand at some proper motor racing that won't break the bank and doesn't demand the skills and experience of Nigel Mansell.

Established back in 1983 by the enthusiastic and dedicated Tim Dodwell, the Road Saloon Register controls a motor racing series that puts an emphasis on fun rather than deadly serious motor sport. Indeed, the element of fun is almost written in to the rules of the Register, and anyone taking the whole thing too seriously is likely to find himself distinctly *persona non grata* with fellow competitors.

This really is the archetypal 'entry level' form of saloon car racing, and will appeal to just about anyone who has ever fancied having a go but has thought either that a) it's too expensive, or b) that as a novice he'll be lost among the ultra professionals and glamorous hotshoes of international motor racing. Tim Dodwell's answer to those questions would be, get along there and have a go — all you'll find is a crowd of people just like yourself, keen to have a good time and enjoy some closely fought but sporting motor racing.

And don't go thinking that the cars you're likely to be competing against are late model, gleaming showroom specials with thousands of pounds lavished on them; think about Minis, and Capris, and SDI Rovers, and RS2000s, and even those classic 'bomb site beauties' from Datsun and Toyota, throw in a few years of hard road use, add a touch of tuning and the obligatory safety fixtures and fittings, and there's your typical Register racer. No different from what you're likely to see parked outside the local autospares accessory shop on any Sunday morning. The difference — and it's a big one — is that the Register racer proves the mettle of *his* car round Brands Hatch, or Snetterton, or Oulton Park, not around the neighbourhood one-way system.

And you don't even have to compete against so-called road cars that in reality are so highly tuned and so modified that they have to be shipped everywhere by trailer. Because, quite simply, trailers —

It's amazing what a few stickers and racing numbers can do for the looks of that old Cortina

and A-frames for that matter – are strictly banned, except for retrieving (heaven forbid) damaged machinery from the circuit after the race. If you're so much as seen with your car on a trailer, or even bring a trailer along to an event, then the Register will reluctantly but resolutely wave goodbye to you as a member. Possibly for ever.

The Road Saloon Register is divided into seven classes which are divided into two groups: the budget-orientated Slick 50 Road Saloons and the more highly modified Super Road Saloons. They are governed by a set of regulations that are both entertaining to read and refreshing in their candour. Any formal regulations that start off:

'*We must stress that you pay careful attention to our rules regarding driving to the circuits, minimal advertising allowed, list of eligible cars and finally our attitude to racing collisions.*

'*Unless you agree totally with all these rules, then we must respectfully suggest that this is the wrong formula for you.*

'*However, if you are in complete agreement, then we would be pleased to welcome you to a superb way of having fun on the racetrack*' just have to have been written by people who live in the real world, not some Cloud-cuckoo-land of theory and red tape.

Below Series founder/organizer Tim Dodwell practises what he preaches in his VW Scirocco

The general rules which define the overall nature of the championships are designed to clarify the attitude of the Register towards its racing. These demand that all cars should be driven all the way to and from (prangs and blowups permitting) race meetings; all competitors should avoid bodywork contact while racing and generally behave in a friendly and sportsmanlike manner; and the first three finishers after every race should allow their cars to be technically inspected if requested.

One problem that can occur in a championship so broadly based is a lack of clear definition as to which cars can be used. The RSR circumvent this by the simple expedient of listing all eligible cars. So if it isn't listed, you can't race it.

At the time of writing the list of eligible cars was as follows:

All cars in the following list, provided that they are in the specification sold in mainland Britain prior to 1 January 1986 and without any optional equipment (unless specifically permitted by the technical regulations).

NOTE All models fitted with more than two valves per cylinder or forced induction are not permitted within the Slick 50 classes.

Cars with locked or limited-slip differentials are not permitted in *any* Road Saloon classes.

Additional cars may be added to the list below at any time at the discretion of the register.

Slick 50 classes

Alfa Romeo Alfasud, Alfetta, Alfa 33, GTV, GTV 6, Giulietta;

Audi 80;

The fact that their race cars have to get them home after the meeting doesn't seem to curb the enthusiasm of road saloon competitors

BMW 2002, 2500, 3.0 (not CSL), 316, 320, 323, 518, 520, 525, 528, 635 (not M635);

Citroen CX, Visa;

Datsun/Nissan Cherry, Bluebird (160B, 180B), 240K;

Fiat 124, 128, 131, Strada, Uno (not spyder versions);

Ford Capri (not RS3100), Cortina, Escort (not RS1600, RS1800, RS1600i, RS Turbo), Fiesta, Granada, Orion, Sierra (not Cosworth versions);

Honda Civic;

Lada 1200, 1300, 1500;

Lancia Beta;

British Leyland etc. Mini, Maestro, Marina, Metro (not 6R4), Montego, Rover 3500S, Rover SDI 3500;

Mitsubishi Colt Lancer;

Opel Commodore, Kadett (not GTE), Manta, Monza;

Peugeot 205, 309, 505;

Renault 5 (not Turbo 2);

Saab 99, 900;

Talbot/Chrysler etc. Avenger (not Tiger), Hunter, Imp, Sunbeam (not Lotus);

Toyota Celica, Corolla;

Vauxhall Astra, Belmont, Cavalier, Chevette (not 2300), Firenza (not droopsnoot), Magnum, Nova (not sport), Viva;

Volkswagen Golf, Jetta, Scirocco;

Volvo 340, 360.

Super classes

Any of the above models, plus any forced induction or fitted with more than two valves per cylinder versions, plus the following models *provided* that full specifications and technical details are available for inspection.

BMW 2002 Turbo, 3.0 CSL, M535i;

Ford Escort Mk III RS1600i;

British Leyland Dolomite Sprint;

Talbot etc. Sunbeam Lotus, Avenger Tiger, Simca Rallye 1;

Vauxhall Firenza droopsnoot, Chevette HS2300 (not HSR), Nova Sport.

Slick 50 Road Saloons The aim here is to achieve a grid of cars that to the casual observer look little different from their everyday shopping counterparts. Indeed, in many cases they are their everyday shopping counterparts, and one can't help wondering if there aren't a few mums and dads around the country puzzled by an uncharacteristic concern for their welfare that has caused their offspring to fit a roll-over bar to the family car. That and the fact that he's booked it in advance for a firm series of Sundays throughout the summer could give justifiable cause for suspicion.

The RSR describe the Slick 50 classification as 'A light-hearted formula for Genuine Roadgoing Saloon Cars from a specified list of eligible vehicles', i.e. those on the list above.

One of the great things about road saloon racing is the variety of cars that take part

Classes are:
1: Up to 1800 cc;
2: 1801 cc to 4000 cc.

Safety regulations demand roll-cage, racing harness, electrical cutout switch and headrest, while a fire extinguisher is recommended.

As for bodywork, this must remain unaltered apart from the driver's seat and steering wheel, although extra instruments (including stereo and speakers!) are permitted if required. You can't even remove the bumpers (that should upset the boy racers) and the only substitution of bodywork material you can get away with is for 'reasonable' repair work.

The engine regulations permit any internal modifications – which, you would be forgiven for thinking, leaves the door wide open for extensive and expensive tuning. But the Register have a way of controlling that because you must use the standard carburettors, standard exhaust manifold and you can't fit a dry sump oil system. This ensures that engine tuning above a certain level is absolutely pointless – spend as much as you like on forged pistons, steel crank, full race camshaft, etc., but the overall power output will be effectively limited by the standard induction and exhaust systems. A neat way of limiting power, and thereby limiting expense.

You can't do very much to the suspension either, except fit uprated dampers – but not the ones with adjustable spring platforms. Nothing else is allowed, except for wheel spacers which, nevertheless, mustn't exceed 3/16 in. wide each side.

Gear ratios are free, and you can alter the internals of the gearbox and differential unit if you wish – but casings and position of gear and differential units must remain the same, and limited-slip or locked differentials are forbidden, even if they are standard fitments.

Naturally no one wants to skimp on safety so brake friction linings can be uprated, Aeroquip-type hoses can be fitted, and the brake backplates can be reshaped to give better cooling. Also you can make any modifications which are hidden by the brake drum. Apart from that, no non-standard parts may be used.

One of the most expensive aspects of motor racing can be wheels and tyres, with a set of light-weight wide alloys and V-rated tyres to suit, sometimes costing as much as £1000, even in some so-called 'low cost' classes of racing. Not so in Slick 50 Road Saloons, however, where you're limited to the standard wheels for the model of car, and tyres only from the Uniroyal range. Tyres can be any size but that doesn't count for a lot when standard wheels are specified.

Remaining detailed regulations cover such aspects as electrics, fuel systems and so on, but the only remaining rules of importance – and they are very significant in terms of controlling the whole nature of the Register – are those which state that cars must be taxed and driven on the road to the circuits, and no advertising is allowed except for a single area on each side of the car of not more than 55 sq. in.

Super Road Saloons This formula is for the more serious competitor who is interested in developing his car and tweaking it up a bit to make it quicker and, perhaps, a shade more exciting to drive. Not that anyone could crave much more excitement than trying to get a virtually standard roadgoing saloon, on standard wheels and tyres, to go round a racing circuit on the outer limits of adhesion. As with the Slick 50 formula the aim is not to encourage people to fling large wads of money at their cars, more to cater for the keen DIY tuner and tinkerer. Also, of course, for the kind of person

who wants to go a damn sight quicker!

Permitted cars are as for the Slick 50 list but with the additions detailed above. Generally, the cars racing in the Super Road series look a bit more like racing cars – but nevertheless retain that essential quality of being road vehicles used on the racetrack rather than vice versa.

All the safety regulations are the same as for the Budget cars, and the usual obligatory RAC MSA requirements apply.

Bodywork regulations are more or less the same as for Budget Saloons, except that wheelarch extensions up to 3 in. either side are permitted, as are front and rear spoilers. Overall the car must remain recognizable as entered.

Engine regulations are rather more liberal, with any internal modifications permitted but this time with free induction systems (so long as the original type is retained, i.e. no turbos replacing carburettors), free exhaust systems and free fuel delivery

Rovers and Capris are popular choices in the big capacity classes

systems (so long as the original type is retained, i.e. no fuel injection if not standard). In other words, quite a high state of tune can be achieved, albeit using fairly straightforward and conventional methods.

Other regulations which differ significantly from the Slick 50 formula are:

Brakes Any substitution of parts is permitted provided they were used in a normal production line car, e.g. you could, if you wished, fit ventilated discs from a 2.8i Capri but you couldn't fit a set of brakes taken from a Williams Formula 1 car.

Wheels Any wheels permitted for racing are allowed. But bear in mind vehicle regulations that forbid wheels extending outside the wheelarches.

Tyres Any tyres listed in the RAC *Blue Book* under Technical Regulations QP 3.1, List 1 – Tyres for Production Saloon Car Racing.

As you can see, the Super Road Saloon regulations permit considerably more in terms of modifications to the standard road car. However, both the Slick 50 and Super formulae provide excellent racing that is right in the heartland of what road car racing is all about, and between them they cater for a wide range of saloon car enthusiasts.

If nothing else it's nice to know that there exists a racing series in which such disparate vehicles as Datsun 240Ks and Rover SD1s can be seen racing together ... or parked side by side in the supermarket car park.

Licence required: RAC Restricted Race with medical examination.

Series co-ordinator: T. Dodwell, 20 The Broadway, Beddington, Croydon, Surrey. Day tel: 01 686 0200. Send s.a.e. if details are required.

Race entry service: The BRSCC, Brands Hatch, Fawkham, Dartford, Kent. Day tel: 0474 874445.

Club membership required: BRSCC Racing Membership; Road Saloon Register membership.

Roadgoing sportscars

Another racing championship organized by the prolific 750 MC, this series is open to genuine roadgoing sportscars as specified in the club's list of eligible cars. Since its conception in 1981 the series has become one of the best supported and friendliest on the club racing calendar, with a wide variety of cars taking part and a sporting atmosphere prevailing among the competitors.

There is quite a wide spread of performance among the cars, with virtually standard cars competing alongside quite highly tuned vehicles, but this seems to work in the series' favour with lots of individual dices taking place throughout the field during most races. One common factor is that all the cars must be fully road legal, with road tax, insurance and a valid MoT certificate regardless of the vehicle's age; this requirement is to ensure that each car is road legal in the eyes of the authorities. MoT certificates must be produced before each race at signing on.

At the time of writing the list of eligible cars was as follows:

Alfa Romeo Spyder and Junior Spyder;
Alpine A110 and A310;
Austin Healey Sprite, 3000, 100/6 and 100/4;
Caterham 7, Super 7 and Super 7 Sprint;
Datsun 260Z and 280Z;
Ferrari Dino 308;
Fiat 124 Spyder and X1/9;
Ginetta G15;
Jaguar E-type and XJS;
Jensen Healey;
Lancia Beta Coupé, Monte Carlo and Celeste;
Lotus Elan, Europa, 7, Esprit and Esprit Turbo;
MG B V8, B GT and Midget;
Matra Baghera and Baghera S;
Mercedes 350SL;
Morgan 4/4, +8 and +4;
Panther Lima and Kallista;
Porsche 914, 911E, 911L, 911S, 911RS, 911RS Turbo, 911SC, 911SC Sport, 911T, 924, 924 Turbo, 928, 928S, 930 and 944;
Reliant Scimitar (all models);
Sunbeam Alpine and Tiger;
TVR 1600M, 3000M, 3500i, Grantura, Griffith, Tasmin, Tuscan, 390SE and 390i;
Triumph Spitfire, Vitesse, Stag, TR2, TR3,

Above **Two Hondas, a Turner and an Elan enjoying a friendly fight at Snetterton**

Right **The Morgan is an evergreen stalwart of roadgoing sportscar racing**

TR3A, TR4, TR4A, TR5, TR6, TR7, TR8 and GT6;
Turner Mk 3.

There are only three capacity classes, which break down as follows:

Class 1: Up to 1300 cc + 0.060 rebore allowance;
Class 2: 1300 to 2500 cc + 0.060 rebore allowance;
Class 3: 2500 cc and over.

Engines with forced induction are subject to an equivalence factor of 1.8:1, thus a 1300 cc turbocharged engine counts as 2340 cc and must compete in Class B.

Basic technical regulations are as laid down in the RAC MSA *Blue Book*, as are the various safety regulations. Unusually the regulations do not

Above **An assortment of roadgoing sportscars squabble for the lead at Silverstone**

Below **A Lotus dices with a TVR at Brands Hatch – the Lotus can also be used in the Lotus/Caterham Seven Championship**

demand the fitment of roll-over bars for closed cars – although they are recommended – but all open cars must have a proper RAC specification roll-bar. Full harness seatbelts are considered a must, as is a 1.5 kg fire extinguisher, a rearward facing red light and an electrical circuit cutout switch.

The chassis must remain as standard and complete, and although material cannot be removed it may be added.

The body must be of generally standard shape with a full-sized windscreen, and full interior trim other than carpets must remain in place. The aim, of course, is to keep the cars looking as much like ordinary road cars as possible, and the forbidding of advertising on the cars helps to enhance this image.

As far as aerodynamic aids are concerned you can only fit rear spoilers, wings or aerofoils if the standard car has them but you can fit a front spoiler provided it doesn't extend beyond the plan view of the car bodywork excluding bumpers.

Engine tuning is pretty free, and you can do more or less what you like provided that the cylinder head and engine block are from the same production car, and bore and stroke remain the same other than the permitted rebore allowance. Cylinder heads with more than two valves per cylinder are only allowed if the head is standard for the car being raced, and racing engines such as Ford FVA/BDA are not allowed.

As for transmissions, the casings must be from a series production car but ratios are free; however, specialist racing gearboxes such as Hewlands are not allowed. The configuration of the power train must remain unchanged from the standard car, which means that although you can swap the type of engine, gearbox, differential and propshaft they have to stay in the same order, e.g. a Triumph Spitfire must retain front engine and gearbox, with propshaft and rear differential – you can't go and insert an Alfetta drive train with rear-mounted gearbox, for instance.

While the suspension must remain of the standard configuration and pick-up points may not be altered, springs and dampers are free so you can have an interesting time playing around with spring and damper rates and ride heights, although at the end of your tweaking and tuning the car must still be capable of passing over a block 3 inches high. To most competitors this is a satisfactory compromise – just enough permitted to make life interesting but not enough to require a vast bank account and a degree in mechanical engineering.

Wheels are limited by width. Tyres must be chosen from those listed by the RAC MSA *Blue Book* under regulation QP 3.1, List 1, Tyres for Production Sportscars.

The 750MC generally has a full calendar of races for roadgoing sportscars at a wide variety of venues, ranging from Lydden Hill in the south-east to Oulton Park in Cheshire, so even if you can't afford to do the whole championship series – or simply don't want to expose your car to too much risk – at least you can take in a limited programme of events at those circuits nearest to you. That way you can get in some exciting and friendly motor racing without overstretching your resources.

Licence required: Restricted Race with medical examination.

Series registration: Dave Bradley, The 750MC, 16 Woodstock Road, Witney, Oxon OX8 6DT.

Club membership required: 750MC.

The 'Mod Prod' saloon series

This relatively new motor racing category is the brainchild of American car racer Brian Sheridan, who launched a 12-round series in 1988 with backing from the Australian 'Truseal' company. The series is now backed by Budget Rentacar International.

Described as a step up from road saloons (see p. 81), the Mod Prod series aims to recreate the 'tin top' racing of the 1970s, with Minis, Escorts, Capris and the big American Camaros and Mustangs all competing together on fairly limited budgets.

Similar in some ways to the two road saloon categories the Mod Prod series, however, insists that cars be trailered to the circuit and permits wheels up to 11 in. wide and tyres up to 10 in. wide.

There are three classes:

Class A: 2401 cc and over, and all turbos, American cars and multi-valves of over 1600 cc;
Class B: 1601 to 2400 cc and multi-valves under 1600 cc;
Class C: Up to 1600 cc.

A list of eligible cars has been produced, and only those on the list will be allowed to compete. The bodyshell must remain virtually standard and unlightened, and all trim and seats must remain in place although the driver's seat may be replaced with a suitable racing version. A driver's headrest of some sort must be provided, which will be no problem if a proper seat is fitted, and all the carpets must be removed to reduce the fire risk. A full roll-cage must be installed, along with full harness belts and a fire extinguisher with a minimum 1.5 kg capacity. A battery cutout switch is also mandatory.

The rest of the regulations allow fairly liberal engine tuning and reasonable suspension modifications and limited-slip or locked differentials are okay in all classes. The big American cars may only use a single four-barrel carburettor, even if original equipment was otherwise, which should prevent the Yanks running away into the distance in every race.

As mentioned before, tyres up to 10 in. wide may be used, and any road legal tyres are permitted – no doubt in the bigger classes wheels and tyres will represent a sizeable chunk of the overall car preparation budget. The final major caveat is that no car should exceed £12,500 in value—to be determined by the race committee.

The following cars are eligible for the series:

Camaro, Mustang, TransAm, Javelin, Barracuda/Charger (up to 5.7 litres), Rover Vitesse, Rover V8, Alfa Romeo GTV6, Capri 3.0S and 2.8i, Sierra XR4i, Escort BDA, Escort RS2000, Escort RS Turbo, Colt Galant Turbo, Nissan 280ZX, Toyota Supra 2.8i, BMW 635 (not CSiA Alloy version), BMW 2002 Turbo, BMW 535 (not M), BMW 325i, BMW 323i, Nissan 240K, Triumph Dolomite Sprint, Lotus Sunbeam, Vauxhall Chevette HS2300 'droopsnoot', Vauxhall Firenza, Opel Monza, Opel Ascona, Opel Manta 2300, Saab Turbo, Volvo 265i, Volvo Turbo, Honda Prelude, Honda Accord 16v, Mazda 626, Fiat Abarth, Fiat Strada, Toyota Corolla 16v, Fiat 132 TC, Jaguar XJ6, Jaguar XJS, Audi GT.

BMW 316, Alfa Giulietta, Escort RS1600, VW Golf GTi, Avenger Tiger, Sunbeam Talbot, Renault 5 Turbo, Lada Samara Turbo, Fiesta XR2, Escort XR3, Capri 1600GT, Toyota Celica 1600ST, Lancia Beta, Fiat Uno Turbo, Metro Turbo, Astra GTE, Peugot 205 GT 1600, Renault Fuego 18GTS, Lotus Cortina, Cortina GT, Scirocco GTi, Hunter 1750, Nissan Bluebird.

MG Metro, Hillman Imp, Ford Fiesta, Toyota Starlet, Vauxhall Viva, VW Polo, Mini, Lada 1300, Lada Samara, Mazda 323, Honda Civic, Peugeot 205, Peugeot 205GTi, Renault 5, Metro, Alfa 1300 Jnr, Lancia Beta 1300, Fiat 128, Opel Kadett, Datsun Cherry.

This series is run by a race committee whose role is to enforce the spirit of the regulations as well as the letter. Budget Rentacar International have injected a big prize fund into the series—£1000 for the winner, £500 for second place, etc.—so it is hotly contested. However, to encourage everyone to have a go £25 travelling expenses will be paid to each competitor at every round, regardless of distance travelled.

Licence required: Restricted Race with medical certificate.

Club membership: BRSCC, Brands Hatch Circuit, Fawkham, Dartford, Kent.

Information pack: Send £5 to Brian Sheriden, Racing Saloon Car Club, 54 Welley Road, Wraysbury, nr Staines, Middlesex. Tel: 0784 813342.

Other possibilities

Other organizations offering championships for roadgoing cars are:

Aston Martin Owners
 Club
J. P. Broadey
Tinnivelli Lodge
Harestone Hill
Caterham
Surrey CR3 6DL

Ferrari Owners Club
 Ltd
J. Swift
145B Leeds Road
Selby
N. Yorks YO8 0JH

Fiat Challenge
A. Andersz
Fiat Autos UK Ltd
Bakers Court
Bakers Road
Uxbridge
Middx UB8 1RG

Jaguar Drivers Club
T. H. Rowe
11 Fairview Road
Timperley
Cheshire WA15 7AR

Morgan Sports Car
 Club
A. Downes
21 Meadow Close
Tring
Herts HP23 5BT

SAAB Challenge
BARC
Thruxton Circuit
Andover
Hants SP11 8PN

Scottish Motor Racing
 Club
A. Mitchell
25 Market Square
Duns
Berwickshire TD11 3ES

Scottish Sporting CC
E. A. Tomney
74 Killermont Road
Bearsden
Glasgow G61 2LS

TR Register
D. Uprichard
Ashdene
Ravenscroft Lane
Beckingham
Doncaster
S. Yorks DN10 4PA

Historic Replicar
Championship
Ron Lea
Meadow End Cottage
53 Marple Road
Charlesworth
Hyde
Derbyshire SK14 6DE

4

Preparation

If you have read the section of this book dealing with the specifications and regulations for the different types of motor sport available to the novice competitor, you will have realized by now that you can't simply take your car straight out of the showroom and compete in an event without carrying out some form of initial preparation.

Now the amount of preparation will differ greatly according to the type of event in question, but as a rough rule of thumb it is true to say that the potentially more dangerous the type of motor sport the greater the amount of preparation that will be required. Thus to compete in autotests or production car trials will require far less preparatory work than circuit racing.

This chapter looks at car preparation in general, and considers all the parts of the car that may require attention; just which of them applies to each individual sector of motor sport depends on the specific regulations, for which refer to Chapter 3.

What we'll do is look at the car in terms of each area and system, and discuss in each case what you *must* do and what you *should* do, which are not necessarily the same thing.

Let's start with the cockpit area. The driver's seat must be firmly fixed in the car so that it can't fold, tilt or recline. This can be a bit of a nuisance if your car is a two-door saloon or 2 + 2 because you will need to tilt the seat forward to let rear seat passengers into the back of the car. If this is the case you've got two options; make your passengers get in on the passenger side, or rig up a device which fixes the seat during racing but which can easily be removed for normal everyday use. Purpose-built racing seats will be fixed rigidly anyhow, but 'sports' type bucket seats or standard production seats will often have a hinged framework which enables the seat to tilt on its subframe. A simple bracket secured by wing nuts can be rigged up to

pinch the rear of the seat frame to its subframe, or for only a few pence you can use a large Jubilee clip for the same purpose.

You must have some form of head restraint for circuit racing, and although it's not mandatory for sprints and hillclimbs I would strongly recommend the same. Whiplash injuries are common enough in low-speed road accidents; combine the speed of motor sport with the increase in weight of your head with a crash helmet on and you have the recipe for very severe neck damage. The easiest way to provide head restraint is by fitting a high-back seat; alternatively you can incorporate a separate padded head restraint into the crossmember of the roll-over bar.

As far as positioning the seat is concerned, the aim is to create a situation of maximum visibility and control. Avoid what seems to be every layman's idea of the ideal racing position like the plague, with the seat so far back and tilted at such an angle that the driver's head is low down in the cockpit and his arms are at full stretch. What you want is to be as upright as possible yet with the controls – foot and hand – within comfortable reach. You must be able to depress the pedals fully without stretching, and your arms should be bent at the elbow so that the wheel can be turned in smooth, supple movements. If you can't grip the top of the steering wheel firmly with both hands while your shoulders are pressed firmly into the back of the seat, then the seat is too far back. Do not underestimate the importance of the correct driving position; it can mean as much as a second per lap.

And if you're going road rallying don't forget the navigator (as if he would let you). He or she must be comfortable, and equipped to do the job required. Basic equipment would include some form of footrest so that the navvy has some means of bracing himself while you're busy whizzing round bends and hanging on to a nice rigid steering wheel. A simple steel tube of 1 inch od welded across the footwell will do the trick nicely. You will also need a Tripmeter (see Chapter 3 on road rallying), a clip to hold the stopwatch (not to mention a stopwatch to go in the clip), a couple of wire pencil holders and – most important – a map reading light. All these goodies can be obtained from your local motor sport accessory shop or by mail order through most of the larger accessory retailers. A torch mounted firmly in a spring clip, a safety warning triangle and a well thought out range of tools should also be readily accessible somewhere within the cockpit area of the car.

On the driver's side, make sure that the pedals lend themselves to swift and easy operation, especially if you use the heel-toe method of changing gear (see Chapter 7). It is no problem bending or adjusting the position of pedals so that your feet don't tie themselves in knots; try to minimize the vertical and horizontal distances your right foot needs to travel between brake pedal and accelerator, but be careful not to get them so close that you end up operating both pedals simultaneously when you least need to.

As far as steering wheels are concerned, don't fit some piddly little 10-inch diameter tiller; it may look fine in a Formula Ford but FFs weigh next to nothing and aren't used on the road. There's no justification for fitting a wheel under 13 inches in diameter, and 14 inches is probably the ideal for most cars. With too small a wheel what you gain in fast response you almost certainly lose in heavy steering and over-sensitivity, which is a real pain during normal road use.

Vinyl-rimmed wheels make your hands sweat more than leather but cost less; if you wear gloves with leather palms you'll get the same grip from vinyl as leather anyhow, so it's a matter of personal choice. Do try to get a wheel with a nice thick rim and padded thumb spats on the spokes though, because then you'll get maximum grip without having to clench your hands; this will give you a more sensitive feel of the steering and will make your steering actions more fluid and precise.

Roll-over bars (or cages) are an essential part of driver safety in any form of motor sport that involves driving at speed; I always reckon that any form of motor sport which involves using more than second gear demands the use of a roll-bar, even when the regulations don't actually insist on

it. The RAC MSA Technical Regulations contain a very detailed section on roll-over structures – Section QM1 – and you should read this carefully. It provides designs for different types of roll-bar, along with material specifications and installation directions. Among the designs are those which are suitable for saloon cars in which a usable rear seat is required; alternatively it is possible to fit a roll-cage which uses detachable diagonal bracing; just remove those intrusive tubes when you're not competing.

Proprietory roll-bars are readily available for most types of car, or you can have one specially made. If you can't afford a tailor-made version, you can install your own. Build your roll-over bar into the structure of the car, welding or bolting it firmly to the chassis or body, using high quality welding or aircraft quality bolts. Various tube materials can be used – alloy, carbon steel, etc. – but the simplest and cheapest is cold drawn seamless carbon steel tube, which should be no less than 38 mm od with a minimum wall thickness of 16 swg. When installed in an open car, the top edge of the roll-over bar should be at least 5 cm above the top of the driver's helmet – a requirement which is not observed often enough in my opinion – and should have at least two back braces to prevent the main roll-over hoop collapsing forwards or backwards.

In certain sprint, hillclimb and autocross classes you can maybe get away with using ordinary lap-and-diagonal seatbelts, but once again I would not seriously consider competing without at least a three-point safety harness. A fairly rudimentary clubman's harness with the two shoulder straps stitched to the lap strap and a simple push-button release can be found for less than £25, or you can spend four or five times that amount on a really pukka aircraft-type harness with all the straps plugging into a quick-release buckle of the highest quality. For sportscars with a semi-reclined driving position I would recommend the use of crotch straps to prevent you 'submarining' out of the seat in the event of a front-on crash, and in all instances you must take great care to ensure that the belt mounting points are securely attached directly to

A well laid out rally car cockpit. Note the easily accessible fuses, padded roll-cage, large warning lights and co-driver's foot brace

the chassis or the roll-over structure.

Full harness belts can be a bit of a liability for everyday use so you may prefer to mount yours on quick release fittings and have an ordinary retractable lap-and-diagonal system permanently in place for normal use. You'll have to check the various makes of harness to see which are available with snap-on hooks rather than more permanent fixings.

When racing it's an advantage to have the seat harness pulled as tight as you can manage. Apart from holding you into the seat and avoiding the necessity of hanging on to the steering wheel in corners it will also help you to become fully attuned to what the car is doing. The more a part of the car you can become the better your driving will be; you and the chassis must function as a single composite unit rather than as two separate entities, and only when you can achieve that kind of harmony will you be able to extract the best performance from yourself and the car.

Even small fire extinguishers carried in a vehicle can contain a fire before it develops seriously. As any car, let alone a motor sport vehicle, is quite capable of bursting into flames for seemingly very

Setting up the engine on a dynamometer can extract horsepower you didn't know you had

little reason, the RAC MSA recommends (and in most cases, demands) that all motor sport vehicles are equipped with at least a 1.5 kg extinguisher.

The extinguishant itself should be of either the BCF (Halon gas) or BTM (gas) type as, obviously, water and certain other types of extinguishant may prove ineffective, dangerous or damaging in fires involving electrical circuitry, petrol, oil, spirit and solvents.

Main rules regarding their use are that they must be capable of being operated by the driver while he is normally seated in the car (with or without harness) either by hand, by contact (i.e. ring pull plumbed-in system) or electrically triggered (i.e. push-button plumbed-in system which may even be linked to heat-smoke sensors). The latter pair can work out expensive but are certainly worth considering in classes where it may take time for help to reach you in the event of a fire if you are incapable of helping yourself. Those which are electrically operated must have their own electrical source completely independent of the vehicle's electrical system to prevent a situation where the car's electrics are damaged and the fire extinguisher is therefore inoperable.

Whichever system you opt for, the extinguishers must be fitted securely within the main structure of the car and not carried loose where they could do more harm than good. They should be capable of being discharged into both the cockpit and the engine compartment, simultaneously if two bottles are carried, which is the maximum number. They should be operable in any position and weighed regularly to ensure their level is sufficient.

If weight-saving is a problem within your car, Dural versions are available to keep extra weight to a minimum, but they aren't cheap. Most race and rally centres will stock these and standard extinguishers in a variety of sizes.

Instruments are very much a case for personal preference, but some categories of the sport demand full standard instrumentation and any road legal car must have a working speedometer at the very least.

Apart from that the most important instruments are: rev-counter, water temperature gauge, and oil pressure gauge. These should be sited on the dashboard in as visible a position as possible. Ancillary gauges such as oil temperature gauge, fuel gauge and ammeter need not be mounted in such a prominent position, and can be sited on a small panel separate from the main dashboard if space is at a premium. If you want to look really professional you can mount the three main gauges in such a way that their needles point directly upwards at the engine's ideal operating performance, so that you can take them in with one glance rather than having to read each dial individually. In other words, if your engine's rev limit is 6000, optimum water temperature is 80 degrees and optimum oil pressure is 60 psi then turn the gauges so that 6000 rpm, 80 degrees and 60 psi are at the top of their respective dials.

Another useful device that's not absolutely

Strut braces not only strengthen the car but also help with handling by preventing chassis flex

necessary but which will be a real boon is a large oil pressure light built into the normal warning system. Something about the size of a Morris Minor rear indicator light is ideal, and will warn you of failing oil pressure when you haven't time to look at the gauges. Many standard oil warning light systems are set at a very low pressure so the engine has probably had it well before the light comes on, but most good racing accessory shops will be able to sell you special competition sender units set at various pressures to suit your particular car.

For speed events you won't need a pukka electrical cutout switch. Simply paint a big directional arrow around the ignition switch and paint the words, 'IGN OFF' next to it; it's also a good idea to write 'IGN ON DASH' (or 'COLUMN' if that's the case) on the driver's door or cockpit edge. For racing and certain other categories, however, you must fit a proper battery cutout switch capable of isolating all the electrical systems. This switch must be accessible from inside and outside the car – easy in an open sportscar, not so easy in a saloon. In the latter case you may have to fit your main cutout switch to the dashboard (or some other convenient point inside the car) and link it by cable to a puller handle outside the car so that a track marshal can cut off the electrics even if he can't get into the car. A choke cable cut to the right length is ideal for this purpose. In both cases the switch and handle must be clearly marked with an 'ON-OFF' sticker and a red spark on a white-edged blue triangle; these are usually supplied in decal form by the switch manufacturer. Cutout switches are available in two configurations: the simplest is an on-off switch which acts as a circuit breaker when let into the battery earth cable. The trouble is if your car is fitted with an alternator the engine will continue to run even with the cutout turned off, so you will have to fit the more expensive variety of switch which can be wired directly into the alternator circuit.

Whatever the type of motor sport the passenger compartment must be isolated from the engine compartment and the fuel tank by flame- and fluidproof bulkheads of non-inflammable material. Quite how one interprets non-inflammable is a moot point, but previous experience suggests that a main bulkhead of aluminium alloy sealed at the edges by grp will do the job to the satisfaction of the scrutineers. Make sure that the bulkheads are properly sealed where cables or pipes pass through; tight-fitting

This kind of fire extinguisher is ideal for motor sport, and is compulsory for many categories. It should be firmly mounted and easily reached by the driver

grommets will probably be acceptable for this purpose.

Final detailing for the cockpit area might include a clutch footrest – easily made with a piece of angled steel or even a spare pedal welded to the floor – and a conveniently mounted pocket to hold a scrap of chamois leather for wiping visor or windscreen while on the move.

Moving on to the bodywork of the car, the most obvious thing you will have to do unless you have a white car is attach white number backgrounds (square or round) for your racing numbers, although some categories settle for black or white numbers on a contrasting background rather than pukka roundels. One on either side and one on the bonnet is the usual requirement. These can be a problem to fit, but there's a neat trick if you want to do it absolutely perfectly with no bubbles. Mix up a foamy solution of washing-up liquid and water and slosh it liberally on to the area where you want to fix the background. Remove the backing paper and apply the circle or square to the soapy bodywork; because it's slippery you will find it easy to manoeuvre into the right position. Then use a sponge or squeegee to press out any bubbles, readjust the position if it has slipped – then simply wait for the soapy water to dry. Result: one perfect number background. This method can, of course, be used for applying any adhesive decals.

All lights, front and rear, must be taped over so that if they get broken they won't drop shards of glass all over the track. A simple crisscross of 'tank' tape over the lamps will do the trick; make sure that each strip overlaps an inch or so on to the surrounding bodywork.

If you're going to be competing in sprints or hillclimbs, where the timing of each run is carried out by breaking a light beam, then a vertical strut must be fitted to the most forward part of the vehicle in order to actuate the light beam. This strut must be opaque and non-reflecting and must be 10 inches high by 2 inches deep and mounted between 8 and 18 inches from the ground.

As far as windscreens are concerned you can use either perspex or glass for racing or speed events. If using a glass screen for racing then it must be laminated glass. If the screen is perspex it must be at least 4 mm thick in all cases, as must side and rear screens although if a sportscar is supplied as standard with plastic sidescreens less than 4 mm thick then they may be retained.

Now let's look at the bonnet and boot area. As I've already mentioned, the fuel tank must be separated from the passenger compartment by a flameproof bulkhead. In addition, if the fuel filler is enclosed within the boot (or within any other part of the car) then a spill collector must be fitted and this must have a vent pipe leading outside the car. In other words, you must rig up a system which prevents any fuel spillage ending up in the car. This doesn't apply if the fuel filler is on the outside, which will almost certainly be the case if you've got

a standard specification car. The only time you're likely to meet this problem is if you fit a special racing tank.

Batteries must be securely fixed so they don't fly around the car, so they can't leak, and so the terminals can't be shorted out. Quite how you do that is subject to interpretation, but I've generally found that as long as the battery is firmly clamped into place the other requirements can be accommodated by attaching a flat rubber sheet (such as a car mat cut to size) over the top of the battery. However, if the battery is fitted in the cockpit of the car it must be enclosed in a leakproof container. Of course, you can get around the leakproofing problem by fitting a dry cell battery if specific requirements permit, but at around £80 they're not cheap.

Within certain limitations the battery is a movable item; so, to a lesser extent, is the fuel tank. They're both quite heavy items so during the planning stage it might be worth giving some thought to their location if the regulations are fairly free. As a rough rule of thumb try to ensure that

An electrical cutout switch is an essential piece of equipment in many motor sport categories

any heavy items are mounted as low down as possible and between the front and rear axle lines. Within those parameters it's best to balance the car as much as possible; for example, if you have a front-engined car then it's a good idea to attempt to move as much weight as you can towards the rear of the car – though without moving aft of the axle line. The three things you're trying to achieve are: a 50/50 fore/aft weight distribution (taking the weight of the driver into account); a low centre of gravity; and low polar moments of inertia. This latter requirement means, in layman's terms, avoiding weight at the extreme front and rear of the car, thereby minimizing the 'dumb-bell effect' in corners, although some drivers (and some cars) perform better with fairly high polar moments.

Within the engine compartment you must ensure that any oil breather pipes that don't return to the engine lead to a suitable catch tank so that oil can't spill or vent on to the track. For speed events the catch tank must be at least 1-litre capacity, whereas for racing it must be at least 2 litres, or 3 litres for engine capacities over 2000 cc. In addition, racing car catch tanks must either be of translucent material or have a transparent inspection panel in them so the contents level can easily be observed. Do make sure that any plastic container you use is capable of carrying hot oil without melting.

Any non-metallic oil or fuel lines passing through the driver/passenger compartment of the car must be of internally or externally metal-braided hydraulic pressure hose, available from any performance-orientated accessory shop or mail-order supplier. The same sort of hose must also be used for carrying coolant.

A point that a lot of novices get caught on is the requirement for 'a positive method of throttle closing, in the event of linkage failure, by means of an external spring to each throttle spindle'. The operative words here are 'external' and 'each'; you can't rely on a concealed spring built into the carburettor, and you must rig up an external spring for each throttle spindle regardless of whether or not the spindles on multi-carburettors are linked by the operating mechanism. Scrutineers love catching people on this one, so be warned.

Left **Full roll-cage, racing seats and full harness seatbelts convert the cockpit into a safety cell**

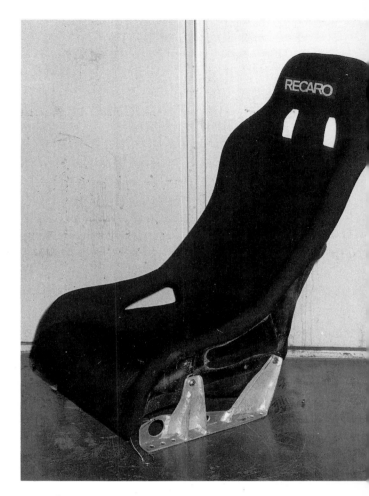

Special competition seats can be a great aid to driving as well as safety

Regardless of any engine tuning you might be doing, fit a brand new set of copper cored HT leads, new points, a 'red top' sports coil and a set of top grade spark plugs; personal favourites are either NGK or Bosch platinum tipped plugs. Mark the plug leads clearly so you can tell at a glance which is which, and make sure they're routed safely away from the exhaust manifold. I once lost a race by a plug lead burning through, and I wouldn't want the same thing happening to you.

Another good 'regardless of anything else' tweak is to fit a proper freeflow air filter if the regulations allow it. And it will do no harm at all to spend a few quid having the engine properly set up on a rolling road dyno just to make sure that everything is working at optimum performance.

Do some testing first to make sure that your car's brakes are up to the increased demands of motor sport and that they don't fade away after a couple of hard applications. Conversely, don't opt straight away for uprated linings; you might well find that in a light car they simply won't reach working temperature. There's a very real danger of reducing the effectiveness of your brakes in this way, especially in short sprints or hillclimbs where the brakes are only used a couple of times per run.

Specially rated springs and adjustable dampers are what you need to fine tune the chassis, but if the cost of them is the difference between competing or not, then by all means have a crack at it using original equipment suspension components. After all, you've got an awful lot to find out about the circuits and your own driving ability before you get into the subtleties of chassis tuning.

As for wheels and tyres, the most important rule here is: don't go too wide. Many categories limit rim widths anyhow. Go too wide and you invite all sorts of handling horrors by altering the suspension geometry, not to mention the extra loading you put on wheel bearings and other suspension components. Besides, tyres operate best at a particular temperature and if you fit extra-wide tyres to a chassis with limited power output the tyres simply won't reach their optimum temperature. As for tyre choice, we'll assume that the car in question is a dual-purpose road/competition car and will therefore use a single type of tyre for both disciplines. If that's the case then you will have to fit tyres listed in the RAC *Blue Book* list of tyres approved for production car racing. As for which of those is the best, that's a decision you'll have to make for yourself, although it may help you to have a look around the paddocks and see what other competitors are using. In fact it's a pretty good idea for any novice racer to have a good sniff around to check out what more seasoned competitors have done with their cars; it can certainly help to short-cut your personal learning process even if it earns you a clip round the ear.

As a final point, do remember to take special care when preparing your car if you intend to use it on the track. Double-check everything, and lock wire or Loctite all important nuts and bolts. Don't take anything for granted and never ever cut corners when fitting suspension, braking and steering components; always use new, top quality components whenever possible.

Oh, and don't worry too much about engine tuning at this stage. The most important thing is to get out there and mix it, learning about yourself and your car at fairly controllable speeds before starting to look for more power. Indeed, an excess of 'grunt' can often prove a handicap to anyone who's really interested in learning to drive properly. Learn how to extract the best out of an underpowered car and you'll have a bit of advantage if you get more bhp at a later date. And you'll have a lot of fun in the process.

What you must do, however, is ensure that your car engine is silenced to the maximum levels laid down in the *Blue Book*, section QA 17; this is something the RAC MSA tends to police quite rigorously.

Finally, don't forget about the competitor – that's you! A crash helmet is required for most forms of motor sport (road rallies, autotests and production car trials being exceptions), but not just any old helmet. Only certain standards of helmet are approved by the RAC MSA and those are the only ones you will be allowed to use. The following standards are okay:

AFNOR S. 72.302/303	DS, SFS, SIS
BS2495 (1977) Amend 5	SNELL 1980
BS6658 – 85 type A	SNELL 1985
ONS DIN 4848	EEC No. 22

Helmets complying with these standards must then carry the RAC MSA approval sticker, which may only be affixed by an RAC scrutineer or by the RAC MSA in Slough. The easiest way to get your helmet approved is to take it along to your first event and have the RAC scrutineer check it over at the same time he looks at your car. Be warned, there is no way you will be allowed to compete in an event which requires a crash helmet if you cannot produce a suitable helmet at scrutineering, either with an RAC sticker already attached or ready to receive one.

Proper fire resistant overalls are mandatory for all circuit races, but are strongly recommended for other categories of racing where fire can be considered a risk. At the very least, the competitor must wear clothing which covers the driver's arms, legs and neck (yes, and the rest of the body as well!)

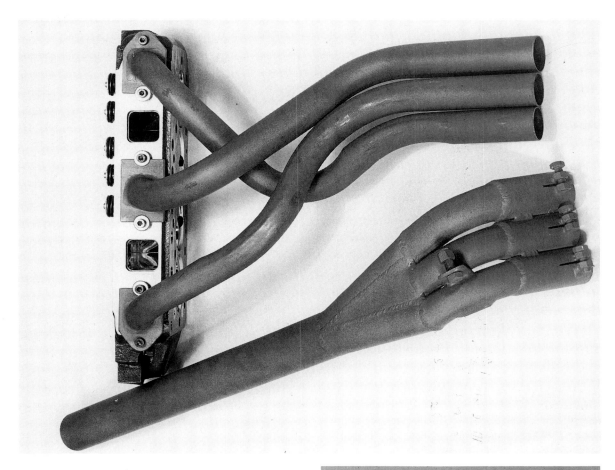

Above Free flow exhaust manifolds can add lots of horsepower for little expense

Right How much is your head worth? When a crash helmet is specified, buy the best

Nylon clothing (particularly underwear and socks) should be avoided as nylon melts when hot and can produce very nasty injuries.

Fire resistant overalls, along with gloves, balaclavas and underwear can provide a very high level of fire resistance but can also cost an awful lot of money. You must assess how great a proportion of your overall budget you can apportion to racewear, and then buy the best you can according to the type of sport in which you are going to compete. It's your body, and therefore it's your risk....

5

Planning and testing

With all the form filling and preparation work out of the way you will no doubt be in something of a hurry to enter your first event. Be patient. Don't rush into it blindly but spend some time familiarizing yourself even more with the *Blue Book* and try to think ahead. Try to plan the events that will make up your season.

It's not a bad idea to draw up some sort of a table which reveals exactly where and when you will be competing and whether or not each event represents a round in a championship. Apart from your own reference, this can also be copied and sent to sponsors, friends and supporters, local newspapers and other interested parties.

It's always hard to know how many events to take in during a season, especially when you're new to the game, but always try to be selective in your choice and realistic as regards how much time and money will be available. For your first season, consider limiting yourself to just one championship, one club or even one circuit in an effort to keep costs down. And don't be caught out by failing to allocate a good proportion of your budget to include test sessions – they may cost more than actual events.

As an example, let's say you plan to do ten events during a season and you've worked out which ones you'd like to do. Now list them in order of importance and tick off the first six as definite dates – perhaps those that make up the rounds of a championship for example. The next two can be listed as probables (perhaps national events towards the end of the season) and two more as possibles (maybe local or one-off events). If everything goes to plan, you can do all ten, but if problems occur (and it would be a rare season if they didn't!) you can reduce your commitment to eight or even six race meetings.

Now add to your list the venues and approximate

dates (just in case sponsors want to attend) for a couple of shake-down practice sessions before the season starts and six or more practice sessions during the season between events and at as many different venues as possible (unless you're limited to a one-circuit championship).

All the major circuits organize open practice days throughout the season, often as regularly as once a week. Telephone the relevant circuit for further details and be aware that the sessions are often subject to reasonable weather, minimum numbers and, sometimes, little more than the whims of the circuit officials. Always book early and confirm that the session hasn't been cancelled by telephoning the circuit before you leave home. Circuits will also want to see your licence and medical certificate so don't forget them.

Open test sessions at a race circuit can be rather unnerving affairs for the uninitiated because there are nearly always hordes of Formula Fords and maybe even Formula 3 machines buzzing around and getting in the way of your Fiat 127 or whatever. The golden rule is, be aware; use your mirrors constantly, give faster cars plenty of room and remember that they are probably travelling twice as fast as you are. You do get used to the blighters, which is just as well because the only way to avoid them is to book a private test session, which costs a fortune. This can be made more affordable if a group of drivers from a club or championship get together to split the cost but it's still much more expensive.

Finding practice time for other forms of motor sport can be more difficult due to a lack of full-time organized venues. Drag strips rarely hold practice days but it might be possible to hire one for the day if you get together with other drivers. Autotesters might be able to find a large tarmac area where they can get permission to practice – it's worth trying some of the companies in your area that have large empty car parks at weekends. Most hill-climbers take their cars to a circuit for setting-up purposes, as do a lot of rally drivers. A word of warning to the rally fraternity – never practice on Forestry Commission land without permission. If you get caught, you can lose your licence for a long time.

I can't really emphasize the importance of test sessions too much. It's a totally different discipline to race driving but it's the great drivers who can do both well. Your early test sessions will provide enough information about yourself and the car to fill a filing cabinet because your learning curve is rocketing through the roof. But as your driving improves and you start to look for those elusive tenths of seconds rather than whole seconds (or even minutes!), testing can become frustrating, infuriating, maybe even tedious – but it never ceases to be a mental and physical challenge. When it all comes together, when you've tried something new and you look at your lap times and you're two-tenths quicker – that's what makes testing so worthwhile.

The first thing to do when you sit in your car for a test session is to get yourself comfortable. Check your controls and safety equipment, adjust your safety harness, your helmet, then try to relax for a minute or two. Think about what you're going to do and ask yourself, 'Does everything feel right?' If it doesn't, your driving will suffer.

Wait for the nod from your mechanic (if you have one) then make your way on to the track for a few easy laps, making sure that everything still feels good. Can you see your instruments? Are the pedals positioned correctly? As you begin to build up speed, ask yourself if the car is behaving itself under braking, cornering and acceleration. Are there any strange noises or vibrations? Why are all the other cars going in the opposite direction?

Now try a couple of faster laps before coming in to let your mechanic take a look at the car for any early warning signs. Even from the very first laps of your very first test session, the most important habit to get into is – *write everything down*. Draw up some simple charts with columns for the date, circuit, weather, track conditions, tyre pressures, suspension settings, lap times etc., with a final column for your own comments or observations.

If you don't record all the data in this way, you really shouldn't waste time going testing in the first place. It might look like a pile of scribble at the time but it's amazing what it can reveal when you analyse the sheets later on. Testing is nothing less than a scientific experiment to discover why you're quicker or slower. These sheets are your proof; without them, all you can really do is guess.

Once you've got the general feel of the car, start to make adjustments as necessary and see what effect they have on your lap times. As a novice driver, be wary of drawing too many firm conclusions from these early sessions because you will undoubtedly get quicker as you gain in confidence. With experience, though, you will learn to drive the car the same way all the time; always taking the same (and hopefully the right) line through corners, knowing when to brake, when to go flat out, when to back off and so on. Soon you'll start to appreciate when you've done a quick lap or a slow one, even though there's less than a second between them, and you'll know that the difference must be because of adjustments made to the car. And because you've written them down, you'll know exactly what they are.

Even experienced drivers, however, find it difficult to detect subtle changes in a car's handling, so don't be afraid to go from one extreme to the other on damper settings, anti-roll bars, tyre pressures etc. to see what effect it has on the car, then work backwards or forwards as necessary. And don't forget that, although there will be some duplication, much of this information will only be relevant for the circuit at which it was obtained. Expecting a car to behave the same at Silverstone as it did at Brands Hatch is asking to be disappointed.

Always try to get something new, to learn something, from every single test session. A race of ten laps is not the best place to make objective observations about the car's behaviour when your adrenalin is pumping and the world has gone mad. Test sessions might be cold, clinical, repetitive, mundane, but they hold the key to winning races. Believe it or not, some drivers claim to enjoy testing *more* than the racing, so try not to think of it as a tiresome chore.

But now the big day approaches. Your first race. You've entered in plenty of time and you've received your passes, entry list and any supplementary regulations. There's your name on the entry list. They've spelt it wrong, but who cares? All you've got to do now is wait, and that's something else you'll need to get used to. Racing drivers tend to do a lot of waiting for something to happen. But when it *does* happen, the wait is always worthwhile.

6

Setting up
by Bob Strange

Bob Strange is Tyre and Vehicle Dynamics Manager for BF Goodrich, and a very successful production car racer. Every year he covers many thousands of miles developing high-performance road tyres and sorting out the handling of his race cars. He is probably one of the most experienced development drivers in the world – and is certainly the most lucid.

Many articles and books have been written that look deeply into the theory of car handling and suspension geometry, and very worthy they are too. However, in this chapter Bob Strange avoids getting bogged down with theory and looks instead at the practical ways of making a car perform better on the road and track.

There is a considerable difference between tuning the suspension of a production car and setting up an outright race car. In most production car categories the regulations restrict you to the original type of suspension, mounted on the car using the original fixing points. And as most production cars have little provision for adjustment you are quite severely limited in how much you can do within a given set of regulations. This means that those things you *are* allowed to adjust and fine tune become very important, especially if you are competing in a category where all the cars are very evenly matched.

The basic concept

Before we get to the practical aspects of tuning a car's suspension, let's consider precisely what it is we are talking about.

There is often confusion among novice drivers over 'roadholding' and 'handling'. Quite simply, 'roadholding' is the amount *of adhesion* the car has on the road surface under braking, accelerating and cornering whereas 'handling' is how the car *behaves* while it is doing those things. For example, a car may have a high level of adhesion but may be a pig to control in the process. It has good roadholding but poor handling. Conversely, another car may not stick to the road very well but may be a delight to drive. In some cases the latter car may actually be the quickest simply because although it may not grip the road as well – perhaps its tyres aren't as 'sticky' – its good handling will provide advantages in other areas, e.g. a better ability to change direction rapidly, less driver fatigue, better straight-line stability, etc.

Other definitions that sometimes confuse are 'understeer' and 'oversteer'. In the simplest terms, understeer means that in a corner the front wheels slide more than the rear wheels, causing the car to try to go straight on. With oversteer the reverse happens, the rear wheels slide more than the front and the car tries to go into a spin. I generally say that with understeer you get to see what you're about to hit whereas with oversteer you don't!

Individual race drivers tend to have their own particular preferences as to how a car handles. Some like a car which oversteers a bit, while others perhaps prefer the car to be fairly neutral, i.e. with no perceptible bias towards oversteer or understeer. This preference will sometimes depend on the type of event, because it is often the case that a car set up for a course with lots of slow, twisty turns will be far less happy on a high-speed circuit with very fast corners.

Perhaps the most important thing to bear in mind when considering a car's roadholding and handling is that the tyres are the car's only point of contact with the road. Whatever you do to the chassis or the suspension it all comes down to the effect it has on those four tiny 'footprints'. And what this means

is that *only the tyres can generate cornering, accelerating or braking forces, because they are the only contact between road and car.* This is a very important concept to grasp, because everything you do to improve the way a car performs has to relate in some way to the tyres; a situation has to be created in which the tyres can perform to the best of their ability.

Ride height

When a car drives round a corner there is a natural tendency for weight to be transferred across the car from the inside wheels to the outside wheels. The more that load is transferred the greater the imbalance between the work that the outside tyres have to carry compared with the inside tyres, and the more we can reduce this transfer the more equally the work will be distributed among all four tyres.

The factor having the greatest effect on weight transfer is the car's centre of gravity; the higher the

A Porsche demonstrates extreme front-end roll stiffness

centre of gravity the greater the load transfer, so if we can lower the centre of gravity we will lower the car's tendency to transfer the load from one side to the other.

The most obvious way to lower the centre of gravity is to lower the car in relationship to its wheels and suspension. This can be done without altering the suspension pick-up points simply by fitting shorter coil springs or fitting lowering blocks between leaf springs and the axle.

An added bonus of lowering the car is the aerodynamic advantage that will be gained by having less airflow under the car. But before lowering your car, check the regulations carefully to make sure that it is permitted; many championships specify a minimum height and you don't want to make your

car ineligible. Apart from which, if you are using your car on the public road you need a certain level of ground clearance if you're not to lose the silencer over every bump.

You must also take great care not to lower the car so much that you run out of suspension travel with the result that the car rides on its bump stops in corners. This has the same effect as suddenly and dramatically increasing the car's roll stiffness, with a consequent fall off in cornering ability.

Roll stiffness

If the centre of gravity determines how much load the car transfers from one side to the other in a corner, the front and rear roll stiffness of the car determines how much of that transfer takes place at the front of the car and how much takes place at the back. In other words, the centre of gravity determines the amount of transfer, the roll stiffness determines where that amount is distributed.

The amount of load that is transferred to the front or rear varies according to the stiffness of the springs, and the rule here is: the stiffest end of the car transfers the load at the greatest rate. Which translates into: the stiffest end breaks away first. So if you stiffen the front end you get more understeer.

When the slip angle of the *rear* tyres is greater than those at the *front*, oversteer is the result. (Photo: *Cars & Car Conversions*)

Let's look at how that works in practice by considering two totally different cars, the Porsche 911 and the Golf GTi.

With the Porsche the rear tyres have to cope not only with the weight of the engine but also with the accelerative forces of the engine, which makes it an inherently oversteering type of car. To reduce that tendency we have to make sure that in cornering most of the weight transfer goes to the front outside tyre – the rear already has quite enough to cope with. So we stiffen up the front end, to the point where – in some cases – so much load is being transferred to the outside front that the inside front wheel lifts right off the ground (see photograph on previous page).

The opposite is the case with the Golf, which is a front-engined, front-wheel-drive car. In this case we want to spare the outside front tyre and load up the outside rear, so we stiffen up the rear end to get maximum weight transfer with the result that Golf GTis cornering with the inside rear wheel in the air are not an uncommon sight.

Now the reason that a car has springs in the first place is to enable the wheels to follow undulations in the road surface and so provide a comfortable ride. If a car had solid suspension it would not only be very uncomfortable but would also leap around all over the place every time it met a bump or pothole, and the wheels would spend more time off the ground than on it. But once you have springs, you have body roll, and the faster you go through a corner the greater the tendency for the body to roll, resulting in unfavourable suspension and camber changes. Which is why one of the first things you do with a car that is to be used for racing is to stiffen up its suspension. The trade-off comes in ride, because the more you stiffen the springs to give better cornering the rougher the ride becomes – something you're going to notice if you are also using your car for everyday road transport.

This is why anti-roll bars can be such a boon, because they enable you to increase the roll stiffness of a car without upping the spring rating. An anti-roll bar links one side of the car's suspension to the other so that load is transferred from one side to the other when the car goes through a corner, but has no effect when the suspension is deflected by bumps. This is particularly beneficial on a road/race car because it means you can run slightly softer springs to give a more pliant ride but also enjoy the benefits of greater roll resistance in corners. And of course you can use anti-roll bars just as you would use springs to control oversteer and understeer.

One thing you have to remember, though, is that anti-roll bars only work if the car is allowed to roll. If you have a car with springs so stiff that it doesn't roll, you can fit anti-roll bars a foot thick and they won't do anything other than increase the weight of the car. We got to that point with the Porsches I race, so we changed to softer springs and a bigger anti-roll bar; the end result in terms of load transfer was the same, but it was a much nicer and easier car to drive.

Wheel and tyre widths

One of the main ways of reducing load transfer under cornering is by increasing the track of the car, which in the case of production car racing means fitting wider wheels and/or increasing the offset of the wheels. The end result is the same, a wider track; but wider wheels (as opposed to merely increasing the offset) also give a bigger 'footprint'

A well scrubbed road tyre is better on dry tarmac than a new, full treaded tyre

on the road and thus greater adhesion capabilities. Wider wheels at the front will reduce understeer, wider at the back will reduce oversteer.

In addition, wider wheels also tend to improve steering response and cornering power because the tyres' sidewalls become more perpendicular with the road surface, which has the effect of stiffening the tyre.

Another advantage comes from improved traction at the driven wheels, with more rubber available to transmit the power to the road.

However, once again there is a trade-off. Wider

wheels transmit more road shocks and put greater stress on suspension and steering components, and if you go very wide you can end up having an effect on the overall suspension geometry that creates more problems than it solves.

Don't forget that as tyres get wider so they get taller, and the taller they get the more sidewall compliance there will be and that will also have an effect on how the suspension performs. Clearly the thing to do is to reduce the aspect ratio of the tyre the wider it gets, but you may be limited here by specific regulations according to the category of sport you have chosen.

Too large a tyre on a small car with low-power output can actually result in slower lap times due to excessive rolling and cornering resistance; in other words a bigger tyre needs more energy to push it along. Also, with a very wide tyre on a very light car you may find that the tyre compound is not getting up to a proper working temperature and a tyre a size or two smaller would be a much better bet.

Static camber

Camber is the angle a wheel leans at from the vertical. Stand in front of a car and look at the front wheels; if they lean inwards at the top then they have negative camber, if they lean outwards they have positive camber. The more a tyre leans the less its 'footprint' is in contact with the road. For a tyre to work to its greatest effect you want the maximum 'footprint' to be in contact with the road, which means that you want the wheel to stay upright as much as possible. Unfortunately, when a car goes round a corner the body rolls and in so doing causes the suspension to tilt which results in wheel camber change. Some suspension systems are designed to compensate for this, but most road cars will finish up with positive camber on the highly-loaded outside tyre. Obviously this means that the tyre 'footprint' is reduced in size and as a result there is less contact between the tyre and the road and a reduction in the amount of cornering force generated. If this loss is greatest at the front, the car will understeer; if greatest at the rear then over-steer will result.

In roadgoing car categories where it is not permitted to alter the suspension geometry the only way to cut down positive camber under cornering is to start out with sufficient static negative camber

Road springs are available in a wide variety of sizes and rates, to enable variations of ride height and stiffness

so that at maximum cornering levels the camber is as near zero as possible.

How much negative static camber you will need depends very much on the individual car, as does the amount of camber adjustment that is available to you. Most road cars have between 2 and 4 degrees of adjustment. I race a production Porsche 944 and would ideally like to dial in $3\frac{1}{2}$ to 4 degrees of negative static camber, but the regulations do not allow it. I have seen people use as much as 5 degrees of negative camber but at the end of the day there's a trade-off, because increased negative camber results in a reduced 'footprint' area in a straight line and under braking, which causes poorer

braking and reduced straight-line stability.

The simplest way of determining how well the tyre is performing with regard to camber settings is by use of a tyre pyrometer, which is a temperature gauge with a probe sensor that enables you to take temperature readings from different parts of the tyre. Put in some quick laps and then immediately sample the temperatures across the width of the tyres. If the outer sector of the tyre tread is significantly hotter than the inner, then the tyre is adopting too much positive camber in the turns; if the inner edge is the hotter then you've dialled in too much negative. Aim for a fairly equal distribution of temperature right across the width of the tread, and you'll have it just right. Not only will you be maximizing the amount of tyre in contact with the road, you will also be avoiding a localized build-up of temperature in part of the tyre.

Of course, if you can't justify the expense of buying a pyrometer for what may, after all, only be

When the slip angle of the *front* tyres is greater than those at the *rear*, understeer is the result – although fairly mild in this case. (Photo: *Cars & Car Conversions*)

a part-time hobby, then you will have to rely on a combination of your 'feel' for the car and carefully documented lap times to get the right settings. Photos of your car in action can also be a help, videos even more so.

Toeing

Imagine you are looking down on a car which is static, in the dead ahead position. It is unlikely that even a standard car will have all the wheels running parallel. If the wheels point inwards at their front edge then they are said to toe in; if they point

This Golf GTi shows the effects of a stiff rear end and softer front. See how the outside front tyre is loaded up, and the inside rear has lifted off the road. (Photo: *Cars & Car Conversions*)

Thick anti-roll bars and uprated springs have virtually eliminated body roll in this TR

outwards they are said to toe out.

Toeing can have a significant effect on vehicle handling. Ideally, maintaining zero toe would allow the suspension geometry to do its job properly. However, there is a certain amount of compliance built into all suspension systems which allows movement of the suspension components within the bushings to absorb shocks. Static toe is added to compensate for this dynamic movement. For example, by toeing-in the front wheels of a rear-drive vehicle the dynamic toeing due to rolling resistance and compliance will be zero.

As a rule, slight toe-out on the front will improve turn-in but it will also make the car rather unstable in a straight line because it's always going to want to turn, it's always going to wander. Suspension systems are designed to initially turn the inside tyre more than the outside when you first start to turn a corner, so although on the face of it you might think toe-in would improve that initial turn-in it is toe-out that will make the car turn in better.

In general I reckon to get as near to zero toeing as possible, perhaps with a little toe-out at the front if the car is a bit slow to turn in. I'm not a big fan of lots of toeing at either end of the car, and if you put toe-out into the rear suspension, especially in a road car that has a lot of compliance, you're really asking for trouble because underbraking the outside tyre is going to want to steer out all the time. And if you're in the middle of a corner and you lift off you're going to get very sudden oversteer. Some people with racing Minis use rear toe-out to help kill the car's inherent understeer, but it makes them impossible to drive under normal circumstances because every time you lift off the thing tries to swap ends.

As a rough rule you can say that toe-in at either end will induce understeer, and toe-out at either end will induce oversteer.

Caster

Of the various aspects of suspension geometry that can be adjusted, caster probably has the least effect on handling. The caster angle affects the car's straight-line tracking and the steering's self-centring effect. The greater the caster angle the more stable the car in a straight line and the less understeer, but it also makes the steering heavier. Very much a matter of how the individual driver likes his car to feel, but I would suggest that the more caster the better until you reach a point where the steering effort is getting out of hand.

Tyre pressures

This is probably one of the most difficult aspects to deal with because so many factors have to be taken into consideration. It is very difficult indeed to recommend specific inflation pressures without a lot of trial and error testing. Among the factors that have to be taken into consideration are suspension type, vehicle weight, weight distribution, drive-axle orientation and driver preference.

As a rule, though, you should aim for the lowest pressure that doesn't generate excessive heat or allow the tyre to roll over on to the sidewall. Too high a pressure is worse for handling than too low, because when you operate a tyre above its optimum inflation pressure the tread stiffens to a point where it loses the ability to conform to the road surface. The result is a loss in cornering power and stability. So if you have a very light car and you are using too high a pressure the tyre tends to run on the centre rather than with the whole width of the tread in contact with the road. If you take temperature samples you will find that the centre is much hotter than the outer edges.

The best way to achieve the correct tyre pressures

Note the different roll characteristics of these two saloons

is by careful testing using a tyre pyrometer. In a production car which you can't modify a lot you will be looking for between 170 and 190° F across the whole width of the tread. But because production cars tend to experience a lot of camber change you won't be able to achieve this, as temperatures will be higher on the outer shoulder. So what you want to aim for is a linear progression of temperatures across the tyre in the range of 160° to 220° F, with the higher temperature experienced on the outside shoulder.

You can generally expect optimum pressures to range between mid-30s psi on lighter vehicles to mid-50s psi on the front of heavier front-wheel-drive cars where handling sometimes has to be sacrificed a little for durability.

Varying the pressures front and rear can alter a car's handling characteristics. The rule of thumb is that reducing the rear pressure increases oversteer, reducing the front increases understeer. This assumes, of course, that the pressures are within the acceptable upper and lower temperature ranges.

All the above factors will affect the handling of the car to a greater or lesser degree, and each will have an influence on all the others. The only way to get your car handling the way you want it is by means of systematic testing against the stopwatch, so that you can confirm that what feels quicker actually *is* quicker.

When you're in the car try to think about what it is actually doing, try to understand what you are having to compensate for. A common trap is to adjust yourself to the car rather than vice versa, compensating for shortcomings in the car rather than analysing what is happening and then trying to sort it out. Every time you drive the car it should be a new learning experience, because a well sorted out car can mean the difference between winning and being an also ran.

When slip angles are equal front and rear, you get a neutral handling car like this. (Photo: *Cars & Car Conversions***)**

7

Driving tips

The coarse racer's guide to competition driving

There have been plenty of manuals written by some very eminent drivers that will tell you all there is to know about the theory and practice of competition driving.

This chapter seeks not to emulate those excellent volumes, but to give an idea of how to cope with some of the realities of competing. Some of the tips described are fairly elementary, others are of questionable legitimacy; what I hope they all have in common is a strong relationship with the real

'Ditch hooking' can have dire consequences if you're not sure what's around the corner

world rather than a set of equations or the subtle niceties of grand prix racing.

It doesn't pretend to be an exhaustive guide, more a list of random thoughts, hints and techniques in no particular order.

First principle Be comfortable. If you are not comfortable you cannot drive quickly or efficiently. When preparing a car for competition it is easy to spend all your time working on different systems of the car while forgetting the most important thing of all, the nut that holds the steering wheel.

The driver's seat should be comfortable and supportive, especially in the lumbar region (the small of the back) and should preferably have a built-in head restraint. In fact seats of this type are a specific requirement in many motor sport categories. If full harness belts are to be used, then a seat with slots to run the harness straps through will be useful. It helps to be strapped as tightly as possible into the seat, which is not possible if the seat prevents the harness straps from laying against your body.

As far as seating position goes, this will depend on the type of motor sport you are contemplating.

Cutting corners may thwart the opposition temporarily, but can play hell with the car's handling. Used with discretion, 'kerbing' can be used to promote oversteer

Autotests and production car trials demand maximum visibility of the car's extremities so a high, commanding driving position will be demanded. For circuit racing a more reclined position may be adopted, while a rally driver will probably prefer somewhere between the two. In categories where competition is against the clock rather than against other cars – drag racing or sprinting for example – all-round visibility is not a priority; the opposite applies for circuit racing.

The cockpit area should be arranged so that the driver is comfortable and can reach all controls with ease. Everything can be adjusted one way or another so there's no excuse for competing in a car that folds you in half or makes you stretch for the gear lever.

The way to set out your cockpit is to start with the factor which is most difficult to adjust then work from there. So begin with the pedals, because they are the most difficult items to adjust to any great degree. Get your seat installed so that you can operate the pedals easily, then fine tune them to suit your own preferences and driving technique by bending or adjusting the levers or welding on extensions.

Now with your seat set so that the pedals can be operated comfortably, you can look at the steering position. Steering wheels with different depths of dish are readily available, and that will give you some scope to get the seating precisely where you want it to provide easy and controlled steering. Avoid being pressed so close to the wheel that you can't operate it smoothly and fluidly; avoid also that awful stereotype of the grand prix driver with his arms stretched at full length. The ideal position enables the driver to grip the top of the steering wheel firmly, with a full fist, without having to lean forward from the seat.

The gear lever will be your next priority, and shortening it, lengthening it or changing the angle of it should be easy enough and should enable you to select all the gears without having to stretch or get involved in weird contortions.

Then you can look at switches and instruments, and with the cornucopia of add-on instrument pods and switch panels adorning the shelves of every accessory shop you shouldn't have too much difficulty getting what you want.

Keep it smooth This is the key to all good driving, on the road or on the track. The car should remain settled at all times – the only time it should be unsettled and unstable is when you have chosen to make it so in order to execute some cunning manœuvre or other.

Avoid sudden transitions, be they from accelerator to brake or from straight ahead to turning. Squeeze the brake pedal, don't stamp on it; accelerate steadily and progressively, not with great blasts of throttle. Don't yank or saw on the wheel, or make alarming stabs at the pedals; the car won't like it. When braking for a corner aim for a swift

Power-induced oversteer can catch you out if you're not careful – and is expensive in rear tyres!

but progressive brake action, followed by a smooth transition from brake to accelerator as you exit the turn. Likewise make the steering progressive and avoid oversteering or over-correcting. When you're driving on the road the car is operating at about five-tenths of its potential so even quite blatant insensitivity won't put it outside its limits. Motor sport creates a whole new problem, because the car will be operating at about eight- or nine-tenths of its potential – sometimes ten-tenths – and your margin for error is much smaller. It's like the difference between walking along a pavement and a tightrope – fine balance and sensitivity is all-important. Try to do everything so smoothly that you can't see the join between one action and the next.

All these considerations are important on dry tarmac – on a wet track or loose surface they are doubly important.

Double de-clutch This section is included at the risk of offending those of you who've been double de-clutching since you first held a provisional licence. If not before.

When changing down a gear at high speed, the moment you let up the clutch in the lower gear the engine is suddenly forced to increase its revs to match the speed of the lower gear ratio. When really pressing on and using the engine as a brake, this can be a sudden and quite violent process unless some effort is made to match the engine revs to the transmission revs before the gear is engaged. This process is called double de-clutching.

It's dead easy, really. Simply press the clutch down; knock the gear lever out of the higher gear and into neutral; let the clutch up; blip the throttle to build up engine revs; depress the clutch; shift out of neutral into the lower gear; and finally let the clutch up again. The secret lies in blipping the throttle by just the right amount, and by carrying out the whole operation so quickly and smoothly that the engine revs haven't died away again by the time you come finally to let out the clutch.

Now by using this method in circumstances where you have to use the brakes as well, for example when slowing down for a corner, you would have to brake first, then come off the brakes to double de-clutch down the gears. Then maybe come back on the brakes again, and even possibly change down again. Wouldn't it be handy if we could operate the brakes *and* double de-clutch all at the same time? Which leads us neatly to the next section.

HEEL-AND-TOE TECHNIQUE

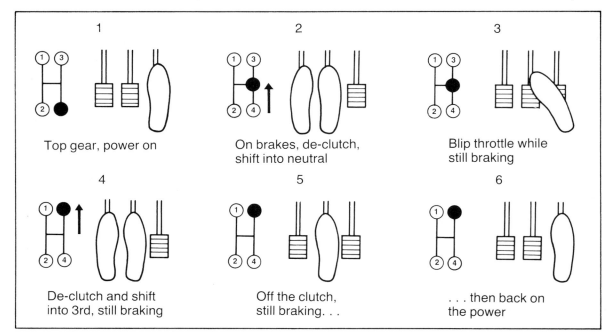

1 — Top gear, power on

2 — On brakes, de-clutch, shift into neutral

3 — Blip throttle while still braking

4 — De-clutch and shift into 3rd, still braking

5 — Off the clutch, still braking...

6 — ... then back on the power

Heel-and-toe Which is something of a misnomer because it generally involves the deft use of the side of the foot rather than the heel, but the expression dates back to the days when pedals were laid out rather differently from today.

Heel-and-toeing is the practice of double declutching while braking. Which, if you think about it, would require us to have three feet. However, by making the right foot perform a dual function we can achieve the same effect. The drawings show how it works (see opposite page).

What you do is brake using the right foot as normal, but place your foot on the brake in such a way that you can rock your foot and use it to blip the accelerator while still braking. Quite which part of your foot operates the accelerator will depend on the layout of your pedals; I've even driven some cars in which I've had to use my ankle bone to blip the pedal. If you're lucky the standard layout of your car will lend itself to heel-toe operation, otherwise you can bend the pedals or fit a short extension to the accelerator pedal.

By using the heel-and-toe technique you can drastically shorten the braking and gearchanging distance, allowing you to brake later and get back on the power sooner. And because the brake is slowing the car down throughout the process it also enables you to change down more than one gear in a single operation – from fourth straight down to second, for example – without destroying the engine or ripping out the transmission in the process.

Cornering, part 1 In the final analysis there are only three types of corner; those at the end of a straight; those at the beginning of a straight; and those that are between other corners, with no perceptible straight either immediately before or after. There are, of course, many subtle variations on those basic themes, but that's what makes it all so interesting.

Let's look at the principles of getting through a corner quickly, by first looking at a corner of constant radius, see Fig. 1. The initial aim is to straighten out the corner as much as possible, i.e. to make its radius as wide as possible. This 'line', which is entirely theoretical, represents the nearest we can get to straightening out the corner without running off the track.

Now, if we assume that all braking and accelerating should be done in a straight line, we can't stay on the brakes after point X, or come on to

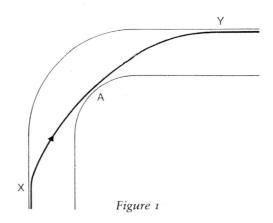

Figure 1

the power before point Y, therefore in theory the section of the corner between X and Y is 'dead' because we are neither braking nor accelerating. And this is wasted area because if we want to be quick we need to be either on the brakes or on the accelerator, not faffing around between the two. So you can see that the straightest way through a corner is not necessarily the quickest. What we have to do is reduce the 'dead' area.

To find out how to do this, let's now take a look at a corner which is followed by a long straight. The aim here will be to get on to the power as soon as possible in order to take maximum advantage of the straight; the earlier you can get on the throttle, the faster your terminal speed will be at the other end. Now look at Fig. 2. By going 'deeper' into the corner before turning we have to make a sharper turn early on but in doing so we can not only brake later but also get on to the power much sooner, because we've made two-thirds of the corner into a straight line. This is known as a 'late apex' corner,

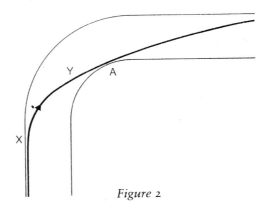

Figure 2

because the apex or 'clipping-point', marked A, comes after the mid-point of the corner.

To see how we take a line through a constant radius corner at the *end* of a long straight, assuming that no straight of any significance follows the corner, look at Fig. 3. In this case you've just spent the distance of the straight building up to top speed and you want to stay at top speed for as long as possible, which means you want to leave your braking as late as possible. So what you do is flatten out the first part of the corner, taking an early apex and leaving the actual turn until the second half of the corner. You can stay on the brakes longer, but the trade-off is that you cannot get on to the throttle until late in the corner.

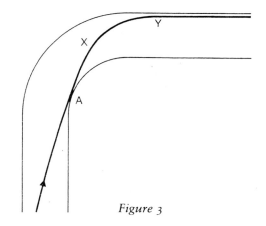

Figure 3

This line, incidentally, is also known as the 'overtaking line' because in circuit racing it is the line you would take to dive up the inside of a competitor and outbrake him into the turn. When overtaking, all the other rules about lines go out of the window.

As mentioned earlier, the third type of corner is the kind that is neither before nor after a straight but is, perhaps, one of a complex of corners. In this case we must look at it with regard to where the next straight is in the sequence, because our aim should be to place ourselves in a situation where we can take the ideal line on to the straight from the last corner in the sequence. Look at Fig. 4, and you will see that the line through the first corner is not the fastest, but it will enable us to place the car in the right position to exit the last corner hard on the power for the following straight.

Corners are seldom of constant radius and each will have to be treated slightly differently. Some

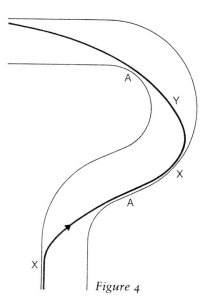

Figure 4

different types of corners are shown in Figs 5, 6 and 7 opposite.

Fig. 5 shows a double-apex bend leading on to a straight, while Fig. 6 shows a double-apex bend leading off a straight; in both cases we can ignore one of the apexes, but the one to ignore differs.

Fig. 7 shows a 'dog leg' corner with a wide section of track leading into a much narrower section. In this case we would take full advantage of the wider part, getting the power on very early and taking a very late apex.

It is important, however, to understand that this is all theory and the reality of the situation may vary somewhat from the textbook technique. Whatever you do don't blindly try to impose rules regardless of any other circumstances. All kinds of things may make the theoretical line impractical; a bumpy surface, oil on the track and above all other competitors – every single factor must be taken into consideration.

Cornering, part 2 While the section above covers the theory of cornering, this bit aims to look at the actual procedure for doing it.

The accepted rule for cornering is to get all your braking, gearchanging and accelerating done in a straight line, which is a reasonable enough thing to tell a novice if you don't want him to get into trouble. It just happens to be not necessarily the quickest way, just the safest.

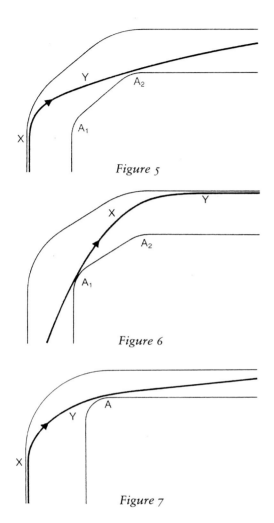

Figure 5

Figure 6

Figure 7

The best way to drive a corner will depend on the car itself and the driver's own preference. Many production cars are set up with a great deal of understeer, because that's reckoned to be the easiest thing to control in an emergency, inasmuch as if the car starts to push straight on in a corner you lift off and it all comes back in line again.

But understeer is the bane of quick cornering. Depending on the regulations for your particular category of motor sport, you may be able to tune out most of a car's inbuilt understeer by tweaking the suspension. But if you can't then you will have a problem when it comes to cornering really quickly. Thankfully there are a number of techniques that you can adopt to make your car turn into a corner much more willingly, even if it's going to revert

back to understeer once it's actually in the corner. In fact, an ideal situation is to have a car that oversteers (or can be made to oversteer) into the bend, and then understeers out.

So how do we get that reluctant car to turn in? One of the most commonly used techniques is **trailing brake**, which spits straight in the eye of the principle of braking in a straight line. What you do is stay on the brakes as you turn into the corner; with the car's nose dipping under deceleration the rear of the car is lighter, the rear tyres are working less efficiently, and it only takes the lateral action of turning into the corner to get the back of the car sliding. This is an excellent way of getting the car to turn in, and with a rear-wheel-drive car the resulting slide can be held on the throttle right through until the car begins to fall back into a neutral or slightly understeering stance as it exits the corner. With a front-wheel-drive car the effect of understeer on the exit can be minimized in this way and the power can be brought in much sooner.

But beware. This technique can just as easily launch you into a violent spin if you are not ultra-sensitive on the pedals and steering, so for heaven's sake don't go practising it on the local ring road.

Also, be sure only to use *trailing* brake; if you try to turn and brake hard simultaneously you will overload the front tyres and cause even more severe understeer than normal.

A rather more brutal way of unloading the rear and making it slide is to drive intentionally on to the inside of the corner. This causes a sudden load transfer from the rear to the front which causes the back to flick out of line. Of course you shouldn't even think about this one unless the kerb slopes fairly gently, but on loose surface events you might find the occasional conveniently sited bump or rut which will enable you to achieve the same effect.

Even more drastic is a technique known among pursuants of off-road motor sport as **ditch hooking**. This involves the rather crass practice of dropping the inside front wheel into any convenient ditch, culvert or rut which happens to lay round the inside of a corner. This tends to 'hook' the car round the corner while at the same time providing a camber advantage by tilting the whole car into the bend. Of course, there is always the danger of choosing a ditch with a large tree trunk or abandoned refrigerator half-way round the corner, which does the front wheel and suspension no good at all....

1

The 'Scandinavian Flick': flick the car left to get the tail sliding (1) then 'pendulum' it the other way (2).

2

Hold the slide round the corner (3) then straighten up as you power out of the bend (4)

3

4

Another way of breaking adhesion on the rear wheels is, of course, by means of the accelerator if the car is rear-wheel drive. A judicious stab on the throttle will get the tail sailing out of line, especially if you have a lot of surplus power on tap. But it's perhaps best if you wait until you have started to turn before gassing it, because if there is lots of surplus power you could find the rear end sliding in the opposite direction to the one you want.

On loose surfaces a variation on the trailing-brake theme is known as the **Scandinavian Flick**, so-called because it was first used by Scandinavian rally drivers. With this technique the car is first set sliding in the opposite direction from the corner, then over-corrected to create a pendulum effect which causes a proportionally much larger slide in the direction you want to go. This method can be fine-tuned to suit any radius of bend, and is particularly useful as a means of getting round tightening radius corners without understeering straight ahead into the undergrowth. Fig. 8 and the photo sequence on pp. 120–1 demonstrate this.

With a front-wheel-drive car you can use 'left-foot braking', another technique perfected by those Flying Finns. As you turn into a corner keep the power on with your right foot but at the same time give the brake pedal a sharp stab with your *left* foot. This will momentarily lock up the rear wheels, while the fact that you've kept the power on will ensure that the front wheels keep turning, and the end result is induced oversteer. Some drivers have got this off to such a fine art that they can drive through a sequence of corners balancing the car simultaneously on the brakes and throttle while making clutchless gearchanges at the same time! Not a technique for the faint-hearted.

'The handbrake turn' is perhaps the best-known technique of all for getting a car to change direction quickly; in its most extreme form it can be used to flick a car through 180 degrees in its own length. The great thing about it is that it's so easy.

Let's assume that we're going to make a sudden sharp turn to the right. In a rear-wheel-drive car, yank the steering wheel round to the right while simultaneously de-clutching and heaving on the handbrake. The handbrake will lock up the rear wheels and the car will execute a wonderfully fast and dramatic spin turn.

In a front-wheel-drive car it's even easier because there's no need to de-clutch, and in fact the power can be kept on to help drive out of the turn.

The ease with which the car turns can be aided by jinking the steering a little to the left before swinging to the right in order to achieve the same sort of pendulum effect which is so essential an ingredient of the Scandinavian Flick.

If you are making frequent use of the handbrake in this way it would be as well to fit a fly-off handbrake conversion, which reverses the ratchet action of the brake and enables you to yank the lever up without the ratchet locking on. Fly-off conversions are readily available from motor sport accessory shops.

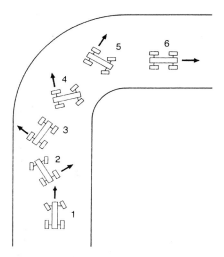

Figure 8 The Scandinavian Flick
(1) From a position roughly midway across the track, flick the car to the left. (2) Catch the resulting slide with opposite lock, but over-correct in order to 'pendulum' the car in the opposite direction (3). (4) and (5) Apply enough opposite lock to hold the slide without spinning the amount of slide you allow will depend on the tightness of the corner

'The reverse flick' is like a handbrake turn but executed going backwards. This is a very dramatic technique that can have dire consequences if not done properly, and by properly I mean with the driver sitting on the outside of the turn rather than the inside. This demands that in a right-hand-drive car a reverse flick should be executed only to the left, so that the weight of the driver will help to prevent the car from flipping over!

This is how it goes in a rear-wheel-drive car; drive briskly backwards then heave the wheel on to right-hand lock while simultaneously de-clutching and yanking on the handbrake. Then wait for the world to stop going round. Again, with a front-wheel-drive car the engine can be used to help the car round. This is definitely the quickest way for a car to swap ends while in reverse, but beware – it can end in disaster.

Yumping Another Scandinavian expression, derived from the Finnish pronunciation of 'jumping'! Only a couple of things to remember if the car gets airborne over a jump: get off the throttle to prevent over-revving, and keep the steering straight. The last thing you want to do is to turn sharp left or right the instant you land; if the corner actually turns left or right immediately after a hump, you shouldn't be flying over it in the first place.

Talking of bumps if you need to use the brakes on a bumpy section of track – and this applies just as much on a race circuit as on an autocross track – try to remember that the car will get lighter as it rises over the bumps and there's a greater chance of locking up the wheels. Leave your braking until you descend into a dip and there will be a greater loading on the tyres as the car suspension compresses, enabling you to brake harder.

A final point Always watch the start of other races when you're at a strange circuit. Look to see where the bottlenecks occur on the first lap because there's often a chance of nipping through on what would normally be a dreadful line, and making up a few places. Conversely, beware of getting trapped in a bottleneck yourself.

There is one thing you can definitely count on: every time you compete you will learn something new. If you're still driving at the age of 80 there will still be a new trick you haven't thought of before, a new technique to perfect. So get out there with your eyes and ears open; learn from books, learn from others – but most of all, learn from yourself.

Yes, this is what we call oversteer! On the racetrack it generally results in slower lap times if it's this extreme

8

Motor racing schools

There are two ways of learning about competition driving: either go out there and have a crack, make your mistakes, maybe bend the car a couple of times and end up much wiser and hopefully better; or shortcut the whole process by signing up for a course at a competition driving school.

While there's a lot to be said for the former approach – and after all, getting out there and competing with your everyday car is what this book is all about – there's nevertheless a lot to be said for taking the benefit of other people's experience.

The possible benefits of a course of instruction fall into three categories. First of all, having a go at a motor sport school in someone else's car within a disciplined environment is a very good way of finding out: a) whether you like it and b) whether you have any aptitude for it. The investment would be less than the cost of preparing your own car, which would be wasted money were you to discover that you didn't like the sport after all.

The second benefit is that of professional driver training, preparing you fully for the time when you come to exercise your skills in your own car. That first event can be a very daunting and nerve-wracking process, but after a motor sport school course you will know much of what to expect and a great deal about how to handle it.

Finally, even if you already have some experience in motor sport a school can be used to refine your skills and add a new perspective to the lessons you have already learned. No one is so good that new light can't be shed on old problems, and even the best sportsmen have coaches and instructors to ensure that the learning process is one of continual growth and development.

Most circuit racing schools provide instruction in their own cars, usually saloon cars for the initial instruction followed by sessions in single-seater racing cars. Rally schools generally provide the vehicles, although if you have your own rally car then most of the schools will be glad to teach you in that. However, the only hillclimb school currently operating in this country demands that you take along your own car.

Instruction techniques vary from school to school, but most of the racing schools start with a brief session in the classroom followed by an on-track assessment to provide the instructor with an idea of each pupil's aptitude. Then it is generally a case of each pupil proceeding at a carefully monitored rate through the various stages of the course.

Although most racing schools offer a full course of instruction taking place over a number of separate daily sessions (taken as frequently as each pupil can manage), they can also be of value on a one-visit basis as a means of becoming familar with driving on a race circuit, which is a very different experience from everyday road driving. If that is what you are after then you will need to look for a school which offers an initial trial in addition to a structured series of lessons.

Rally schools, on the other hand, tend towards the complete, self-contained single-day or weekend session, while the hillclimb school only operates on a one-day basis.

Even if your particular branch of the sport doesn't fall directly into the category of race, rally or hillclimb, a course or single session at an appropriate school can teach some valuable lessons that will be relevant to any category of the sport.

Racing schools

Aintree Racing Drivers School
7 Andrew Close
Tarvin
Chester CH3 8LN
0829 41513

Brands Hatch Racing
Brands Hatch Circuit
Nr Dartford
Kent
0474 872331

Tom Brown Racing School
Knockhill Racing Circuit
Dunfermline
Fife KY12 9 XX
0383 723337

Mark Cole Racing
Castle Combe Race Circuit
Castle Combe
Wilts.
9702 218799

Everyman Motor Racing Ltd
128A Alcester Road
Moseley
Birmingham B13 8EE
021 449 9351
(Mallory Park Circuit)

Jim Russell International Racing Drivers School
Snetterton Circuit
Norwich NR16 2JX
095387 8428

Silverstone Racing School
Unit 22
Silverstone Circuit
Towcester
Northants

Ian Taylor Racing School
Thruxton Circuit
Andover
Hants
Weyhill 3511

Team Touraco International Racing Drivers School
Unit 2 Warwick Road
Fairfield Industrial Estate
Louth
Lincs.
0507 602944/5

Rally schools

Bill Gwynne Rally School
Unit 7 Thorpe Place
Overthorpe Rd Industrial Estate
Banbury
Oxon.
0295 51201
(Operates at Turweston, nr Brackley)

Rally School Ltd
The Studio
Silverstone
Northants
0327 857413
(Operates at Bruntingthorpe, Leics.)

RSD
1 Orchard Rise
Olveston
Bristol
Avon
0454 613394
(Operates at Llandow, S. Wales)

Welsh Forest Rally School
Cambrian House
Carno
Caersws
Powys
05514 201
(Operates in the Hafren/Dyfnant/Dovey area)

Hillclimb schools

Prescott Hillclimb School
The Bugatti Owners Club
Prescott Hill
Gotherington
Nr Cheltenham
Glos.
GL52 4RD

Index

References to illustrations appear in italics.